WILLIAMS-SONOMA

NEW FLAVORS FOR
desserts

RECIPES
Raquel Pelzel

PHOTOGRAPHS
Tucker + Hossler

Oxmoor
House®

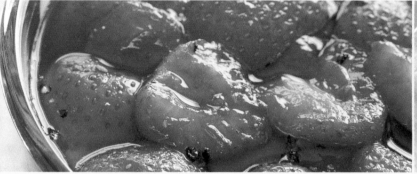

spring

summer

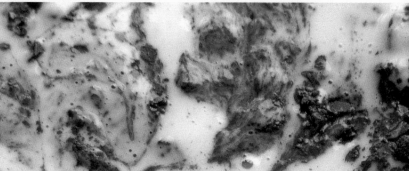

fall

winter

introducing new flavors

In today's global community, we have access to a whole world of alluring ingredients, such as spices, herbs, chocolates, and liqueurs, that are sourced from all over the earth. At the same time, the local and seasonally driven food movement has brought supreme-quality ingredients into our kitchens from nearby farms and growers. In a delicious new way, we can pair once-exotic flavorings with local, farm-fresh ingredients to reinvigorate our favorite recipes. High-impact elements add bold bursts of flavors and a layering of textures and tastes create dishes that truly engage the senses. This is the essence of these dessert recipes.

Inspiration to bring fresh flavor and personality to your cooking and baking can be found just about everywhere—in a well-stocked grocery store, at a farmers' market, at a local cheesemonger, in a specialty spice shop, and in your own herb garden. Look to nature for ideas and guidance: What's ripest, freshest, and most flavorful is the produce that is in season locally and is in abundance at the farm stand. Then, as you cook and bake, add flavorings with a bold, adventurous spirit, reinventing old favorites with new, exotic tastes.

Seasonally organized, this book features forty-four dessert recipes, each one thoughtfully crafted to take advantage of fruit and produce at the pinnacle of freshness. The recipes are seasonally minded in other ways—light, fresh, and grilled desserts are for warm weather and long days; hearty, soul-warming ones for chilly months. In every season you will find sumptuous, inviting desserts that are new, yet somehow familiar. With each flavorful bite, they will delight your palate with comforting flavors, and surprise with unexpected twists.

freshness as an ingredient

The most important ingredient in these recipes is not butter, or sugar, or even flour. It's freshness. Fresh ingredients—whether dairy, spices, or fruits—are the keys to full flavor because they're sweet, pure, and intense. With freshness as the main ingredient, everything that follows is purely icing on the cake.

seasonal The fruits that fill the farmers' market at the height of their harvesting seasons are naturally plump and sugary, and their colors are rich and saturated. But appearance doesn't tell all. Take a whiff—a sweet, heady perfume should flood your senses. With such honeyed ambrosia and character, peak-season fruit is easy to showcase in a simple dessert. Let the seasons be your cue: There's no better time for a peach cobbler than the summer, or the autumn for roasted pears.

local Try to buy your ingredients from a nearby farm stand or farmers' market. From local sources, it's likely that the cherries in the pint-sized container and the plums in the wooden crate were picked only hours earlier by people with a genuine interest in the quality of the produce. Because they have very little distance to travel from farm to table, most locally grown fruits can stay on the tree until they're fully ripened. This translates to sweeter, more delicious flavor.

organic Choosing organic fruits over conventional ones is another way to guarantee freshness. Organic produce isn't treated with the synthetic pesticides and preservatives that conventional produce is. So, while conventional produce has a long shelf life, its flavor can wane without notice, but short-lived organic produce has a natural peak that you're forced to catch—and enjoy.

being bold

The recipes in this book capture bold, exciting flavors and introduce them to classic desserts. They feature high-impact ingredients with unique character and flavor-intense foods from the international pantry. The recipes also draw inspiration from the savory side. The results are delicious revelations: globally influenced desserts that are brimming with fresh, innovative tastes.

high-impact flavors With intensity of flavor built in, dessert is a memorable event, not just a conclusion to a meal. In these recipes, bold accents come from spices, herbs, and cheeses, as well as from more surprising sources such as tea leaves, extra-virgin olive oil, and even sea salt. The secret to integrating these big flavors into desserts is to balance them with the other components in the dish.

global ingredients The world market brings a fresh direction to the realm of dessert. International ingredients, such as Italian balsamic vinegar, Chinese five-spice, and imported wines and spirits, can instantly add a modern twist and an element of adventure to classic desserts. Finding these ingredients has never been easier, thanks to well-stocked grocery stores and specialty food shops.

unexpected combinations Savory underpinnings and unusual pairings of flavors bring an element of surprise to desserts and give them an edge that tastes fresh and new. Goat cheese and lemons, rosemary and Port, and basil and melon are all unexpected combinations that, when brought together with a little sugar, are turned into enticing desserts that awaken the palate. A bold spirit is all that it takes to create surprisingly delicious treats.

flavors in layers

A balance as well as a contrast of flavors, textures, and temperatures has been carefully considered to create complexity within each dessert in this book. Overlapping layers build desserts that intrigue the palate from the very first taste.

taste Combining contrasting taste elements, like hot with sour, is by no means a new concept. In desserts, however, using savory ingredients such as pungent black peppercorns or salty *fleur de sel* is a fresh idea that adds depth and dimension. When the flavors are layered, sweetness is the first sensation on the palate, and from there, the flavors blossom in surprising ways, creating a deliciously complex dessert.

texture Complementary textures in desserts make them especially satisfying—a crisp sugar crust offsets a silky custard filling and crunchy graham cracker crumbles counter the fluffiness of a mousse. Adding texture can be as easy as a sprinkle of toasted nuts or a dollop of whipped cream, but it's a thoughtful touch that can elevate a dessert from simple to sublime.

temperature Matching cold components with warm ones creates a comforting effect as well as a range of sensations that keeps the palate engaged. With a contrast in temperature, such as a scoop of cold ice cream on a warm fruit crisp, a simple dessert is inviting and enticing from the first bite to the very last.

Making classic desserts taste unique and inspired does not always mean making them complicated. In fact, simplicity is key: With the finest, freshest ingredients as a starting point, and lush, bold flavors as seasonings, a mundane dessert is easily transformed into a memorable grande finale.

spring

cardamom-spiced mango pavlovas

large egg whites, 4, at room temperature

cream of tartar, ⅛ teaspoon

sugar, 1¼ cups

cornstarch, 1 tablespoon

whole green cardamom pods, 20

mangoes, 3

lime, 1

sweetened whipped cream (page 144)

MAKES 6 SERVINGS

Preheat the oven to 275°F. Line a rimmed baking sheet with parchment paper. Using a stand mixer on high speed, beat the egg whites until foamy. Add the cream of tartar and continue to beat while gradually adding ¾ cup of the sugar until soft peaks form. Sift the cornstarch over the whites and gently fold it into the mixture.

Spoon 6 dollops of the mixture, now called a meringue, onto the prepared baking sheet, dividing it evenly and leaving a few inches between each one. Using the back of a spoon and working in a circular motion, spread each dollop into a disk about 4 inches wide and make a depression in the center of each. Bake the meringues until they are no longer tacky on the surface and are very lightly golden, about 1 hour. Let the meringues cool completely on the baking sheet on a wire rack.

Using the flat side of a chef's knife, lightly crack open the cardamom pods. Add the pods to a saucepan along with the remaining ½ cup sugar and ⅓ cup water and bring to a simmer over medium-high heat. Simmer, swirling occasionally, until the sugar is dissolved, about 2 minutes. Let cool to room temperature.

Peel the mangoes, cut the flesh into ½-inch cubes, and add the cubes to a bowl. Using a zester, remove some of lime zest in thin strips and set aside for garnish. Squeeze the juice from the lime over the mango, pour the cardamom syrup through a fine-mesh sieve into the bowl, and mix well.

To serve, place each of the meringues on a dessert plate. Spoon a generous amount of whipped cream on top of each meringue. Using a slotted spoon, top the whipped cream with some of the mango cubes. Drizzle a little cardamom syrup over the top, garnish with the lime zest strips, and serve right away.

Cardamom is wonderfully complex in flavor. The tiny, sticky seeds inside the fibrous husks contain hints of ginger, allspice, clove, and black pepper, with a unique brightness. In this recipe, a syrup spiced with cardamom perfectly complements the tropical sweetness of creamy-textured mangoes.

white chocolate trifle with strawberries and pineapple

White chocolate has a buttery taste with subtle hints of vanilla. In this simple trifle, its richness strikes a delicious balance with the tart acidity of fresh fruit and the bite of dark rum. A sprinkling of toasted coconut adds nuttiness and a crisp, yet chewy, texture.

Add the white chocolate to a large heatproof bowl. In a saucepan over medium-high heat, bring the cream to a simmer. Pour the hot cream over the chocolate, cover, and set aside for 5 minutes. Uncover and whisk until melted and smooth. Refrigerate the chocolate mixture, stirring it every 10 minutes, until cooled but not firm, about 30 minutes. Whisk the whipped cream into the cooled chocolate. (If the chocolate is too stiff, let it soften at room temperature before mixing in the whipped cream.)

Finely grate the zest from the lime, then squeeze the juice. In a nonreactive saucepan, combine the lime zest, lime juice, ginger, ¼ cup water, and the sugar. Bring to a simmer over medium-high heat, swirling occasionally, until the sugar is dissolved, about 2 minutes, then continue to simmer until bubbly, 1–2 minutes longer. Let cool to room temperature.

Add the pineapple and strawberries to a bowl. Measure 3 tablespoons of the ginger-lime syrup into a small bowl, add the rum, and stir to combine. Pour the remaining syrup over the fruit and toss well.

Arrange a layer of ladyfingers in the bottom of a 3½- to 4-quart straight-sided glass bowl, breaking up the cookies as needed to fill any gaps. Brush the ladyfingers with rum syrup until soaked through but not falling apart. Spoon one-half of the fruit mixture over the ladyfingers and cover with one-half of the white chocolate cream. Repeat with one more layer each of ladyfingers, syrup, fruit, and white chocolate cream. Cover with plastic wrap and refrigerate the trifle for at least 2 hours or up to overnight.

When ready to serve, sprinkle the trifle with the toasted coconut. Use a large spoon to scoop portions of the trifle onto small plates.

white chocolate, 1 pound, finely chopped

heavy cream, 1 cup

sweetened whipped cream (page 144)

lime, 1

fresh ginger, one 2-inch piece, peeled and grated

sugar, 2 tablespoons

pineapple, 1, peeled, cored, and finely diced

strawberries, 2 pints, hulled and finely diced

spiced dark rum, ⅓ cup

crisp ladyfingers, 35–50, depending on size (about 7 ounces total weight)

unsweetened coconut flakes, 1½ cups, toasted (page 94)

MAKES 10–12 SERVINGS

Brown butter used in place of regular butter in a simple pound cake lends a full, nutty taste. Instead of finishing with a glaze, pair the cake with a quick-cooked compote of spring's brightly flavored rhubarb and juicy fresh strawberries.

brown butter pound cake with strawberry-rhubarb compote

Brown butter has the taste and aroma of toasted hazelnuts and boasts a fuller, deeper flavor and color than plain butter. Here, it enriches a plush pound cake with a nuttiness that is set off by a simple sweet-tart compote.

Preheat the oven to 325°F. Grease a 9-by-5-by-3-inch loaf pan with butter. Melt the 1 cup butter in a saucepan over medium heat. Reduce the heat to medium-low and gently simmer, swirling the pan often, until the butter is browned and smells nutty, 12–15 minutes. Strain the butter through a fine-mesh sieve and let cool to room temperature.

In a bowl, whisk together the cake flour, baking powder, and ½ teaspoon salt. Using a stand mixer on medium-high speed, beat the whole eggs, egg yolks, 1 cup of the sugar, and the vanilla until pale and thick, 2–3 minutes. Reduce the speed to low and add the dry ingredients in 2 batches, mixing until only a few streaks remain. Raise the speed to medium-low and drizzle in all but 2 tablespoons of the brown butter. Raise the speed to medium and beat until combined. Scrape the batter into the prepared pan.

Bake the cake for 40 minutes, rotating it halfway through baking. Brush the top with the remaining brown butter and sprinkle with the 1 tablespoon sugar. Continue baking until a cake tester inserted into the center comes out clean, 10–15 minutes longer. Let the cake cool in the pan on a wire rack for 30 minutes. Turn the cake out onto the rack and let cool completely.

In a nonreactive saucepan, combine 3 tablespoons of the orange juice, the remaining ⅓ cup sugar, and a pinch of salt. Bring to a simmer over medium-high heat. Add the rhubarb, bring to a boil, reduce the heat to medium-low, and simmer, stirring occasionally, until softened, about 5 minutes. Add the strawberries and simmer until softened, about 2 minutes. In a small bowl, mix the arrowroot and the remaining 1 tablespoon orange juice and stir into the rhubarb mixture. Let cool to room temperature.

To serve, slice the cake, divide among plates, and top with the compote.

unsalted butter, 1 cup, at room temperature, plus butter for greasing

cake flour, 1¼ cups

baking powder, ¼ teaspoon

salt

large eggs, 3, at room temperature

large egg yolks, 2, at room temperature

sugar, 1⅓ cups, plus 1 tablespoon for sprinkling

pure vanilla extract, ½ teaspoon

fresh orange juice, 4 tablespoons

rhubarb stalks, ½ pound, cut into ¼-inch slices

strawberries, 2 pints, hulled and quartered

arrowroot, 1½ teaspoons

MAKES 8 SERVINGS

grilled spiced pineapple with cinnamon-spiked ice cream

sugar, 1 cup

ground cinnamon,
2½ teaspoons

ground allspice,
¼ teaspoon

ground cloves, ⅛ teaspoon

pineapple, 1

high-quality vanilla ice cream, 1 pint

dark spiced rum, ¾ cup

MAKES 6 SERVINGS

Soak 6 bamboo skewers in water to cover for at least 30 minutes. In a small saucepan, combine ½ cup of the sugar, ⅓ cup water, 1 teaspoon of the cinnamon, the allspice, and cloves and bring to a simmer over medium-high heat. Simmer, swirling occasionally, until the sugar is dissolved, about 2 minutes. Let cool to room temperature.

Using a chef's knife, peel the pineapple, cut it lengthwise into eighths, and cut away the tough core from each piece. Cut each pineapple spear crosswise into 1-inch chunks. Drain the skewers, then thread the pineapple onto them, dividing the chunks evenly.

Prepare a gas or charcoal grill for direct-heat grilling over medium-high heat. While the grill is heating, line a large rectangular, airtight container with plastic wrap. Scoop out 6 evenly sized balls of ice cream and place in the prepared container. Cover and keep in the freezer while you grill the pineapple. Pour the rum into a shallow bowl and place in the freezer as well. In a small, shallow bowl, mix together the remaining ½ cup sugar and the remaining 1½ teaspoons cinnamon.

Brush the pineapple skewers with the spiced syrup, coating the pineapple chunks well. Grill the pineapple until lightly charred on all sides, 4–6 minutes total. Slide the pineapple from the skewers into 6 bowls.

Remove the ice cream balls and rum from the freezer. Dip one of the ice cream balls into the rum, then dip one side into the cinnamon-sugar mixture. Place the ice cream, spiced side up, on top of the pineapple. Repeat with the remaining ice cream balls and serve right away.

Earthy, woodsy cinnamon is a spicy flavor accent for smoke-tinged pineapple and creamy vanilla ice cream. The combination of warm grilled pineapple and cold spiced ice cream creates a pleasing contrast of temperatures in this easy-to-make dessert.

Buttermilk takes the place of milk or cream in the filling for these three-bite tartlets, yielding a lighter version of a classic custard tart. Baked in muffin cups, the tartlets form whimsical flower-like shapes that are perfectly suited to spring.

buttermilk tartlets with fresh spring berries

all-purpose flour

basic tartlet dough
(page 142)

buttermilk, 1½ cups

heavy cream, ½ cup

fresh lemon juice,
2 teaspoons

sugar, 1 cup

cornstarch,
1½ tablespoons

salt, pinch

large egg yolks, 2, at room
temperature

unsalted butter,
1 tablespoon

fresh berries, such as
raspberries or strawberries,
½ pint

MAKES 12 TARTLETS

Position one rack in the lower third of the oven, another rack 3–4 inches below the heating element, and preheat the oven to 375°F.

On a lightly floured work surface, roll out the dough into a 12-inch circle about ¼ inch thick. Prick the dough all over with a fork. Using a 3½-inch round pastry cutter, cut out 12 circles. Gently press each circle into a cup of a 12-cup muffin pan (the dough will not reach the top of the cup) and freeze for about 30 minutes. Bake the tartlet shells on the lower rack until they turn a light golden, 12–15 minutes. Let the tartlet shells cool completely in the pan on a wire rack.

In a nonreactive saucepan, combine the buttermilk, cream, and lemon juice. In a small bowl, whisk together the sugar, cornstarch, and salt. Add the sugar mixture to the saucepan along with the egg yolks and whisk to blend. Cook over medium heat, whisking constantly, until the mixture reaches a simmer and is as thick as pudding, about 6 minutes. Strain the mixture through a fine-mesh sieve into a large liquid measuring cup, then whisk in the butter until blended.

Pour about 2 tablespoons filling into each tartlet shell. Bake the tartlets on the lower rack until the filling is dry on top but still jiggles slightly in the center when gently shaken, about 15 minutes. Preheat the broiler, transfer the tartlets to the upper rack, and broil until the tops are spotty brown, about 1½ minutes. Let the tartlets cool in the pan for about 5 minutes, then transfer them to the wire rack and let cool completely.

To serve, top the tartlets with berries and arrange on a platter or plates.

Buttermilk's tanginess is tempered by the richness of egg yolks and heavy cream in these miniature tartlets. The tartlets' subtly sweet, lemon-kissed flavor lets the fresh, juicy late-spring berries that top them really sparkle.

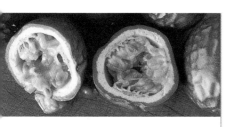

passion fruit cupcakes with coconut frosting

The pulp of passion fruit is intensely sweet-and-sour and has a fruity, exotic taste with hints of citrus and flowers. In this recipe, rich, vanilla-scented cupcakes are filled with a sunny-colored passion fruit curd and are finished with a sweet coconut frosting that pairs perfectly with the cupcakes' tropical flavor.

Preheat the oven to 375°F. Spray a 12-cup muffin pan with nonstick cooking spray and place a cupcake liner in each muffin cup. In a bowl, whisk together the flour, baking powder, and salt. Combine the cream and vanilla in a liquid measuring cup.

Using a stand mixer on low speed, beat ¾ cup of the butter and the granulated sugar until blended, then raise the speed to medium-high and beat until light and fluffy, 1–2 minutes. Beat in the eggs, 1 at a time, scraping the sides of the bowl after each addition. Reduce the mixer speed to low and add the dry ingredients in 3 batches, alternately with the cream mixture in 2 batches. Scrape the sides of the bowl. Raise the mixer speed to medium-high and beat for 1 minute to aerate. Divide the batter evenly among the muffin cups. Bake until the centers spring back when pressed lightly with a fingertip, about 20 minutes. Let the cupcakes cool in the pan for 10 minutes, then transfer to a wire rack and let cool completely.

Using a stand mixer on medium-low speed, beat the remaining ½ cup butter with half of the confectioners' sugar until crumbly. Add the remaining confectioners' sugar and beat until powdery, about 1 minute. In a liquid measuring cup, whisk together the coconut milk and extract. With the mixer on medium speed, slowly add the coconut mixture and beat until blended. Raise the speed to medium-high and beat until light and fluffy, about 1 minute.

Using a paring knife, cut a 1½-inch-wide cone-shaped core halfway down into the center of each cupcake; gently remove the cores and set aside. Fill each cupcake with about 1 tablespoon of the passion fruit curd and replace the cores. Frost the cupcakes with the coconut frosting and sprinkle with the chopped nuts. Let the frosting set for about 15 minutes, then serve.

nonstick cooking spray

all-purpose flour, 1¾ cups

baking powder,
2 teaspoons

salt, ½ teaspoon

heavy cream, 1 cup, at room temperature

pure vanilla extract,
1 teaspoon

unsalted butter, 1¼ cups, at room temperature

granulated sugar, ⅔ cup

large eggs, 2, at room temperature

confectioners' sugar,
3¾ cups

unsweetened coconut milk, ⅓ cup

coconut extract,
1 teaspoon

**passion fruit curd
(page 143)**

macadamia nuts, ½ cup, finely chopped

MAKES 12 CUPCAKES

gingered rhubarb crisp

rhubarb stalks, 1½ pounds

oranges, 3

granulated sugar, 1 cup

fresh ginger, one 3-inch piece, peeled and grated

all-purpose flour, 1½ cups

light brown sugar, ¾ cup firmly packed

quick-cooking rolled oats, ½ cup

ground cinnamon, ½ teaspoon

salt, ¼ teaspoon

unsalted butter, 6 tablespoons, melted

high-quality vanilla ice cream for serving

MAKES 8 SERVINGS

Preheat the oven to 375°F. Cut the rhubarb into ¼-inch slices and place in a 13-by-9-by-2-inch baking dish. Finely grate the zest from 1 of the oranges and add it to the dish. Squeeze ⅔ cup juice from the oranges and add to the dish along with the granulated sugar. Toss the rhubarb mixture with your hands, then spread it out evenly in the baking dish.

In a bowl, combine the ginger, flour, brown sugar, oats, cinnamon, and salt. Using a fork, toss until blended and then stir in the melted butter until the ingredients are evenly moistened.

Sprinkle the oat mixture over the rhubarb and bake for 15 minutes. Loosely cover the baking dish with aluminum foil and continue to bake until the topping is browned and the juices are thick and bubbling around the edges of the dish, 15–20 minutes longer. Let the crisp cool, uncovered, on a wire rack for at least 20 minutes.

To serve, spoon the warm crisp into bowls, top with scoops of ice cream, and serve right away.

A generous amount of freshly grated ginger adds a warm, spicy bite to this otherwise classic crisp. Blended into a buttery oatmeal topping, the ginger is an exotic partner to the rhubarb's bright flavor. As it melts onto the warm crisp, cold vanilla ice cream ties all the tastes together and offers a nice contrast in temperature and texture.

Apricots and almonds, a delightful pairing, are a perfect match in a dessert for late spring. In the rustic free-form tart that follows, their subtle flavors are made sweeter and more intense by the addition of sugar and the heat of the oven.

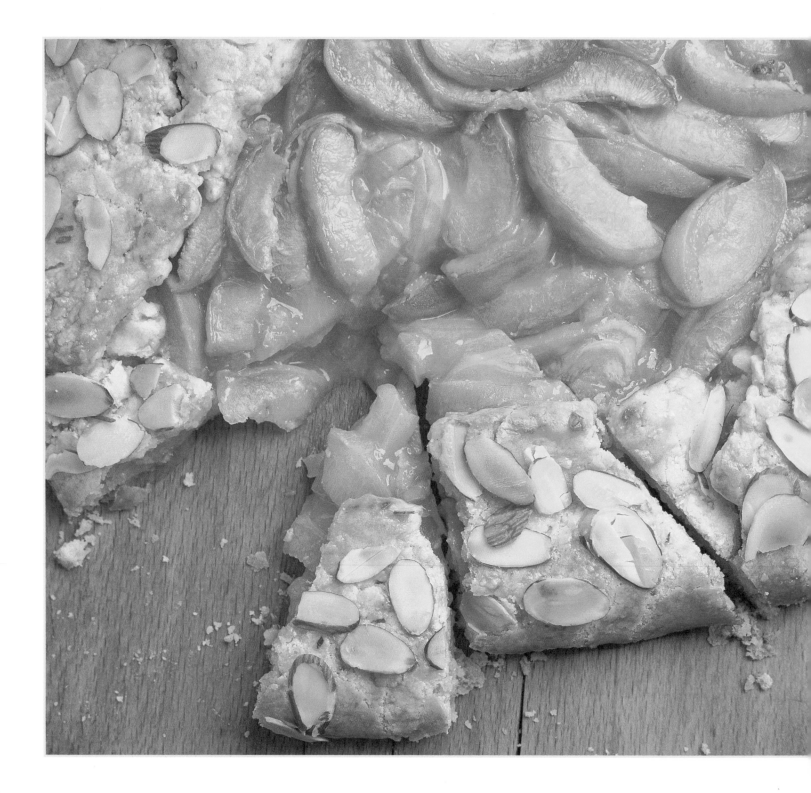

apricot and almond galette

apricots, 1½ pounds

fresh lemon juice,
1 tablespoon

sugar, ½ cup

all-purpose flour

**almond galette dough
(page 142)**

apricot jam or preserves,
⅓ cup

large egg, 1

sliced almonds,
3 tablespoons

MAKES 6–8 SERVINGS

Preheat the oven to 375°F. Line a rimmed baking sheet with parchment paper. Halve, pit, and thinly slice the apricots, then add them to a bowl along with the lemon juice and sugar. Toss to coat the apricots well.

On a lightly floured work surface, roll out the dough into a 15- to 16-inch round about ¼ inch thick. Fold the dough into quarters and unfold it onto the prepared baking sheet. Spread the apricot jam over the dough, leaving a 3-inch border uncovered, then arrange the apricots evenly on top of the jam. Fold the dough edges over the apricots, loosely pleating the dough and leaving the galette open in the center.

In a small bowl, whisk together the egg and 1 tablespoon water. Brush the dough with the egg mixture and sprinkle with the almonds.

Bake the galette until the dough and almonds are browned and the apricots are tender when pierced with a knife, 35–45 minutes. Let cool completely on the baking sheet on a wire rack.

To serve, transfer the galette to a platter or cutting board, cut it into wedges, and divide among serving plates.

Almonds bring both their nuttiness and sweetness to this charming open-faced tart in two ways: Ground almonds are mixed into the dough and sliced almonds are sprinkled over the tart edges before baking. The rich, tender pastry is a buttery envelope for plump, fragrant apricots that have an affinity for earthy almonds.

key lime—cocoa tartlets

Key limes are small in size, but they're full of citrusy fragrance and have a uniquely sharp acidity. For these tartlets, they're made into a sweet yet tangy filling with a color and taste that contrasts with the bittersweet cocoa crusts. A rich crème fraîche topping tames all the bold flavors.

Preheat the oven to 375°F. Pat the dough into a 6-by-9-inch rectangle. Cut the rectangle in half lengthwise, then cut each half crosswise into thirds; you should have six 3-inch squares. Place each square in a 3-inch tartlet pan, then dip your fingertips in cocoa powder and press the dough into the bottom and up the sides of the pans. Press off any excess dough from around the edges of the pans, and use any scraps to fill cracks or holes. Place the tartlet shells on a rimmed baking sheet and bake until set, about 10 minutes. Let the shells cool on the baking sheet on a wire rack.

Meanwhile, in a bowl, whisk together all but 3 tablespoons of the sweetened condensed milk (save it for another use if desired), the whole egg, egg yolks, and rum. Finely grate the zest from 3 of the limes, then squeeze ⅓ cup lime juice. Whisk the lime zest and juice into the condensed-milk mixture. Ladle the filling into the tartlet shells, dividing it evenly, and bake until just set, about 15 minutes. Let cool to room temperature on the baking sheet on a wire rack, then cover with plastic wrap and refrigerate for at least 4 hours or up to 2 days.

When ready to serve, spread about 1½ tablespoons crème fraîche over the top of each tartlet, leaving a narrow border around the edges. Finely grate a little chocolate over the tartlets, remove them from their pans, and serve.

cocoa tartlet dough (page 142), at room temperature

unsweetened cocoa powder

sweetened condensed milk, 1 can (14 ounces)

large egg, 1, at room temperature

large egg yolks, 2, at room temperature

white rum, 3 tablespoons

key limes, 7–8

crème fraîche (page 144 or purchased), ⅔ cup

bittersweet chocolate for garnish

MAKES 6 TARTLETS

jasmine-scented tapioca pudding with kiwifruit

large pearl tapioca, 1 cup

whole milk, 4 cups

sugar, ¼ cup

half-and-half, ¾ cup

loose-leaf jasmine tea, 2 tablespoons

fresh kiwifruit, 3

MAKES 6 SERVINGS

Place the tapioca in a large bowl, cover with 3 inches of cold water, and soak overnight at room temperature.

In a large saucepan over medium-high heat, combine the milk and sugar and bring to a simmer. Drain the tapioca, add to the milk mixture, and stir to blend. Reduce the heat to medium and simmer, stirring often, until the tapioca is tender, 20–25 minutes. If the mixture begins to boil, reduce the heat to medium-low. Drain the tapioca, reserving 1 cup of the cooking liquid. Let the cooking liquid cool, then refrigerate, covered, until needed.

While the tapioca is cooking, in a small saucepan over medium-high heat, bring the half-and-half to a simmer. Remove from the heat, add the jasmine tea, cover, and let steep for 5 minutes.

Pour the tea-infused half-and-half through a fine-mesh sieve into the drained tapioca and stir to blend; discard the tea leaves. Let the tapioca mixture cool to room temperature, then refrigerate for at least 3 hours or preferably overnight.

When ready to serve, peel the kiwifruit, cut them lengthwise into quarters, then cut the quarters crosswise into ½-inch-thick pieces. Thin the pudding to the desired consistency with the reserved cooking liquid. Spoon the pudding into bowls, top with the kiwifruit, and serve.

Jasmine tea infuses this pudding with a delicate floral aroma and light herbal nuances, while large pearl tapioca gives it a distinctive look and unique texture. Fresh kiwifruit adds vibrant color and brings a tart fruitiness that balances the pudding's richness.

Freshly cracked black pepper adds subtle spiciness to plump strawberries and dark, syrupy balsamic vinegar echoes the berries' sweet-tart taste. The delicious result is surprising dessert of layered flavors and an intensified strawberry essence.

strawberry parfaits with black pepper and balsamic vinegar

black peppercorns,
2 teaspoons

strawberries, 2 pints

sugar, 1/2 cup

high-quality, aged balsamic vinegar, 2 tablespoons

kirsch, 1 tablespoon

high-quality vanilla ice cream, 1 pint

sweetened whipped cream (page 144)

MAKES 6 SERVINGS

Using a mortar and pestle or spice grinder, roughly crack the black peppercorns. Hull the strawberries and halve about half of them lengthwise. Place all the strawberries in a bowl and add the cracked pepper.

In a heavy saucepan, combine the sugar and 1/4 cup water. Cover and bring to a simmer over medium heat, checking the sugar often. Once the sugar starts to melt, uncover and swirl the pan occasionally until the sugar is dissolved, about 5 minutes. Continue to simmer, uncovered, until the sugar turns to a deep amber brown caramel, 3–5 minutes longer.

Carefully add the strawberry mixture to the caramel (it will fizz vigorously and harden in spots). Using a heatproof silicone spatula, stir the berries into the caramel as best you can and cook, stirring often, until any hardened bits of caramel have melted, 1–2 minutes. Transfer to a bowl and mix in the balsamic vinegar and kirsch. Let cool to room temperature, then cover with plastic wrap and refrigerate for at least 1 hour or up to 8 hours.

When ready to serve, let the ice cream stand at room temperature for about 10 minutes to soften slightly. Layer the ingredients in 6 stemless wineglasses or parfait glasses in this order: strawberries with juices; ice cream; more strawberries with juices; and finally whipped cream, dividing the elements evenly. Serve right away.

Zesty black pepper and molasses-like aged balsamic vinegar meld with ripe, fresh late-spring strawberries for an intensely flavored dessert. A layer of rich vanilla ice cream mellows the assertiveness of the ingredients and rounds out the dish.

summer

chocolate-espresso torte with fresh sour cherries

unsalted butter, ½ cup, at room temperature, plus butter for greasing

bittersweet chocolate, ¾ pound, finely chopped

unsweetened chocolate, ¼ pound, finely chopped

brewed espresso, ½ cup, at room temperature

pure vanilla extract, ½ teaspoon

salt, ½ teaspoon

large egg yolks, 6, at room temperature

sugar, 1 cup

large egg whites, 4, at room temperature

cream of tartar, ¼ teaspoon

fresh sour cherries, ¾ pound

cherry juice, ⅓ cup

arrowroot, 1 tablespoon

brandy, 2 tablespoons

MAKES 8–10 SERVINGS

Preheat the oven to 400°F. Grease a 9-inch springform pan with butter, line the bottom with a parchment-paper circle, and grease the parchment with butter. Wrap the outside of the pan with a large sheet of aluminum foil.

Melt the ½ cup butter and the chocolates in a heatproof bowl set over (but not touching) simmering water in a saucepan; stir often until smooth. Stir in the espresso, vanilla, and salt. Set aside to cool slightly.

In a large bowl, vigorously whisk the egg yolks with ½ cup of the sugar until pale and creamy, then fold in the chocolate mixture. Using a stand mixer on medium-high speed, beat the egg whites and cream of tartar until foamy. Slowly add ¼ cup of the sugar and beat until the whites hold stiff, shiny peaks. Gently fold the egg whites into the chocolate mixture and scrape the batter into the prepared pan. Place the springform pan in a large roasting pan, place in the oven, and pour about 1 inch of very hot water into the roasting pan. Bake for 10 minutes, reduce the heat to 350°F, and continue baking until the center of the torte is set, 25–30 minutes longer.

Remove the torte from the water bath, discard the aluminum foil, and let cool on a wire rack for 1 hour. Remove the springform pan sides, then invert the torte onto a greased sheet of parchment paper. Lift off the pan bottom, peel off the parchment circle, turn the torte right side up onto a cake plate, and let cool completely.

Pit and halve the cherries. In a saucepan, combine the cherries, cherry juice, and remaining ¼ cup sugar and bring to a simmer over medium-high heat. Simmer, stirring occasionally, until the cherries soften slightly, 1–2 minutes. In a small bowl, mix the arrowroot and brandy and stir into the cherry mixture. Transfer the mixture to a bowl and let cool completely.

Slice the torte into wedges and serve with the cherry topping.

The smoky flavor of espresso is an exceptional match for bittersweet chocolate, and this dark, decadent torte showcases their perfect marriage. A sour cherry topping is a foil for the torte's richness and its ruby-red color provides a stunning visual contrast.

cornmeal shortcakes with fresh blueberries and sweet cream

With the addition yellow of cornmeal, simple shortcakes gain hearty texture and a nutty flavor that pairs perfectly with blueberries. The berries' fruitiness is intensified by gently cooking a portion of them until juicy and then mixing in fresh berries for texture. Soft, fluffy, vanilla-scented whipped cream pulls all the elements together.

Preheat the oven to 400°F. Line a rimmed baking sheet with parchment paper. Pour 4 pints of the blueberries into a large bowl. In a saucepan, combine the remaining 2 pints blueberries, the sugar, and lemon juice. Cook the berries over medium heat, stirring occasionally, until most of the berries have burst and are very juicy, 8–10 minutes. Pour the warm blueberry mixture over the fresh blueberries, stir gently to combine, and set aside.

In a large bowl, whisk together the 2 cups flour, the cornmeal, baking powder, and salt. Add the butter pieces to the bowl. Using your fingertips or a pastry blender, work the butter into the dry ingredients until the texture resembles coarse meal. Drizzle in the cream and stir with a wooden spoon until evenly moistened. The dough should be moist and cohesive. If the dough looks and feels dry, stir in more cream, 1 tablespoon at a time, until it comes together.

On a lightly floured work surface, pat the dough into a round about ½ inch thick. Using a 3-inch pastry cutter, cut out as many rounds as possible, then place on the prepared baking sheet. Bring the dough scraps together and repeat; you should have 8 rounds total. Reduce the oven temperature to 375°F and bake the shortcakes until golden brown, 16–18 minutes. Let cool completely on the baking sheet on a wire rack.

Using a serrated knife, halve the shortcakes horizontally. Place the bottom halves, cut sides up, on dessert plates. Spoon about 3 tablespoons of the blueberry mixture on the bottoms, then spoon dollops of whipped cream on top of the berries. Cover with the top halves of the shortcakes, cut sides down, and serve right away.

blueberries, 6 pints

sugar, ½ cup

fresh lemon juice, 1 tablespoon

all-purpose flour, 2 cups, plus flour for dusting

yellow cornmeal, ⅓ cup

baking powder, 2 teaspoons

salt, ½ teaspoon

cold unsalted butter, 10 tablespoons, cut into ½-inch pieces

heavy cream, 1 cup, plus cream as needed

sweetened whipped cream (page 144)

MAKES 8 SERVINGS

Emerald-green basil and juicy cantaloupe are both at their peak at the height of summer. An odd couple, perhaps, but in an icy granita, they are deliciously harmonious, with each flavor accentuating the refreshing qualities of the other.

cantaloupe-basil granita

Fresh basil, with its anise undertones, is unusual to find in desserts, but in this icy granita, basil pairs perfectly with musky ripe cantaloupe. The result is a bracing dessert that's full of fresh, but earthy, flavor. Because the ingredients are so few, be sure to use the finest-quality produce to make the best-tasting granita.

Coarsely chop 20 basil leaves; set the remaining 10 leaves aside. In a small nonreactive saucepan, combine the lime juice, sugar, and 2 tablespoons water and bring to a simmer over medium-high heat. Simmer, swirling occasionally, until the sugar is dissolved, about 2 minutes. Remove from the heat, stir in the chopped basil, cover, and let steep for 15 minutes.

Meanwhile, halve the cantaloupe and scoop out and discard the seeds. Cut away the rind and cut the melon flesh into 1-inch cubes.

Strain the basil mixture through a fine-mesh sieve into a blender. Add half of the melon cubes and pulse a few times, then purée until smooth. Add the remaining melon cubes and pulse a few times, then add the remaining whole basil leaves and purée until the mixture is smooth. Pour the mixture into a 13-by-9-by-2-inch glass baking dish, cover with plastic wrap, place on a rimmed baking sheet, and place in the freezer.

After 1–1½ hours, check the granita. When the mixture starts to freeze around the edges of the dish, stir it with a fork, then return the dish to the freezer. Stir the granita every 45 minutes until the grains are completely frozen and the texture is fluffy, about 2–3 hours longer.

Spoon the granita into serving dishes and serve right away. (The granita is best when eaten within 2 days. If it becomes very hard and dry in the freezer, let it sit at room temperature for 10–15 minutes before serving.)

fresh basil leaves, 30

fresh lime juice, ¼ cup

sugar, ⅔ cup

ripe cantaloupe, 1 (about 4 pounds)

MAKES 8 SERVINGS

vanilla-pluot coffee cake with walnut streusel

cold unsalted butter, ½ cup plus 3 tablespoons, plus butter for greasing

cinnamon sticks, 2

vanilla bean, 1

all-purpose flour, 2 cups

granulated sugar, ½ cup plus 3 tablespoons

dark brown sugar, ½ cup firmly packed

ground cinnamon, ¼ teaspoon

walnut pieces, ½ cup

pluots, 3

fresh lemon juice, 2 tablespoons

baking powder, 1½ teaspoons

baking soda, ¼ teaspoon

salt, ½ teaspoon

sour cream, ¾ cup

large eggs, 2

pure vanilla extract, ½ teaspoon

MAKES 8 OR 9 SERVINGS

Preheat the oven to 350°F. Grease an 8-inch square baking dish with butter.

Melt the ½ cup butter in a saucepan over medium heat. Add the cinnamon sticks, reduce the heat to medium-low, and gently simmer, swirling the pan often, until the butter is browned and smells nutty, 12–15 minutes. Strain the brown butter through a fine-mesh sieve into a bowl. Discard the cinnamon sticks. Using a paring knife, cut the vanilla bean in half lengthwise and scrape out the seeds. Whisk the vanilla seeds and bean halves into the butter. Let cool to room temperature.

Meanwhile, to make the streusel, in a bowl, combine ½ cup of the flour, 2 tablespoons of the granulated sugar, the brown sugar, and ground cinnamon. Add the 3 tablespoons cold butter and work it in with your fingertips until the mixture resembles coarse meal. Stir in the walnut pieces and set aside.

Halve, pit, and finely dice the pluots and add them to a bowl. Add the lemon juice and 1 tablespoon of the granulated sugar and toss well.

In a large bowl, whisk together the remaining 1½ cups flour, the remaining ½ cup granulated sugar, the baking powder, baking soda, and salt. Remove and discard the vanilla bean from the brown butter, then whisk in the sour cream, eggs, and vanilla extract. Pour the butter mixture over the flour mixture and stir until just combined. Spread the batter in the prepared pan, top evenly with the pluots, and sprinkle with the streusel.

Bake the cake until golden brown and the center resists light pressure, 35–45 minutes. After 25 minutes of baking, if the topping looks dark, loosely cover the cake with aluminum foil and continue to bake. Let the cake cool in the baking dish on a wire rack for at least 30 minutes, then cut into squares and serve.

A pliant, plump vanilla bean is full of heady aroma, with delicate nuances of flowers and almonds. In this recipe, a vanilla bean and pure vanilla extract infuse their intoxicating essence into a rich coffee cake that is accented by sweet-tart pluots and a buttery walnut streusel.

Lemongrass is often used in savory stir-fries and curries, but its fresh, clean flavor is also at home in desserts. Citrusy lemongrass-infused sugar syrup subtly sweetens fragrant, ripe raspberries. The light lemon hints heighten the berries' rosy flavor.

raspberries in lemongrass syrup

fresh lemongrass, 1 stalk

sugar, 1/3 cup

raspberries, 4 pints

sweetened whipped cream (page 144) for serving

MAKES 6 SERVINGS

Remove the dry outer leaves of the lemongrass and then trim the stalk to a 3-inch piece of the pale green bottom section. Using the back of the blade of a chef's knife, bruise the lemongrass, flattening the stalk and breaking some of the fibers to release its aroma.

In a small saucepan, combine the sugar and 1/3 cup water and bring to a simmer over medium-high heat. Simmer, swirling occasionally, until the sugar is dissolved, about 2 minutes, then remove from the heat. Add the lemongrass, cover, and let cool completely, about 30 minutes.

Strain the lemongrass syrup through a fine-mesh sieve into a large bowl, pressing on the stalk with the back of a spoon to extract as much syrup as possible; discard the lemongrass.

Add the raspberries to the syrup and gently stir. Divide the raspberries and syrup among 6 bowls. Top with the whipped cream and serve right away.

This new spin on the classic pairing of berries and cream captures the mild lemony essence and herbal nuances of lemongrass and pairs it with juicy raspberries. It's a nearly effortless way to show off the floral fragrance and taste of ripe red raspberries.

white peach cobbler with crystallized ginger

Crystallized ginger sparkles with the peppery heat of fresh ginger, but with a pungency tamed by sweetness. Tiny bits of it baked into the biscuit topping add an unexpected chewiness and spiciness that enhances fragrant white peaches. The juicy cobbler filling is seasoned with grated fresh ginger for added dimension.

Bring a large pot of water to a boil. Preheat the oven to 375°F.

Meanwhile, fill a large bowl with ice water. Score an X into the bottom of each peach. A few at a time, drop the peaches into the boiling water and cook briefly until the skins begin to split and loosen, 15–60 seconds, depending on the ripeness of the fruit. Using a slotted spoon, transfer the peaches to the ice-water bath to cool.

Peel, halve, pit, and slice the peaches and place them in a large bowl. Finely grate 2 teaspoons zest from the lemon, then squeeze 2 tablespoons lemon juice and add both to the peaches. Add the grated fresh ginger, granulated sugar, cornstarch, and a pinch of salt to the peaches and toss gently.

In a food processor, combine the 2 cups flour, the baking powder, and ½ teaspoon salt. Add the crystallized ginger and pulse briefly to combine. Add the butter to the food processor and pulse until the mixture resembles coarse meal. Transfer the mixture to a large bowl, add the 1¼ cups cream, and mix until the dough comes together. Turn the dough out onto a lightly floured work surface and knead 2 or 3 times to bring the dough together into a ball. Shape the dough into a round about ½ inch thick, then use a knife to cut the dough into 8 even wedges.

Transfer the peach mixture to a 13-by-9-by-2-inch baking dish and arrange the dough wedges on top in 2 rows of 4, alternating the points. Brush the wedges with cream and sprinkle evenly with the turbinado sugar. Bake for 25 minutes. Loosely cover the baking dish with aluminum foil and continue to bake until the topping is deep golden brown and the juices are bubbling, 10–20 minutes longer. Let cool, uncovered, for at least 20 minutes.

To serve, spoon the warm cobbler into bowls, top with scoops of ice cream, and serve right away.

white peaches, 10

lemon, 1

fresh ginger, one 1½-inch piece, peeled and grated

granulated sugar, ⅓ cup

cornstarch, 2 tablespoons

salt

all-purpose flour, 2 cups, plus flour for dusting

baking powder, 2 teaspoons

crystallized ginger, ½ cup, coarsely chopped

cold unsalted butter, 4 tablespoons, cut into ½-inch pieces

heavy cream, 1¼ cups, plus cream for brushing

turbinado sugar, ¼ cup

high-quality vanilla ice cream for serving

MAKES 8 SERVINGS

blackberry summer puddings

brioche, 1 loaf (1 pound)

blackberries, 4 pints

sugar, ¾ cup

salt, pinch

lime, 1

crème fraîche (page 144 or purchased) for serving

MAKES 6 SERVINGS

Preheat the oven to 250°F. Cut the brioche into twelve ½-inch slices. Using a 3½-inch pastry cutter, cut out circles from 6 of the slices. Trim the crusts off the remaining 6 slices. Place the 6 circles and 6 slices on a baking sheet and bake until dry, 1½–2 hours.

In a nonreactive saucepan, combine the blackberries, sugar, and salt. Finely grate 1 teaspoon zest from the lime and squeeze 1 tablespoon lime juice and add both to the pan. Cook the blackberry mixture over medium heat, stirring occasionally, until about half of the berries have burst, 8–9 minutes. Drain through a fine-mesh sieve set over a bowl for 10 minutes.

Meanwhile, line six 3½-inch ramekins with pieces of plastic wrap long enough so the sides hang over the edges by about 3 inches.

Remove the sieve with the berries from the bowl and set aside. One at a time, lightly soak the bread slices in the berry juices until the bread is soft but not falling apart. As each slice is soaked, place it in one of the prepared ramekins, pressing it into the corners and up the sides. If the bread breaks apart, just push it together. Divide the berries among the bread-lined ramekins. Lightly soak the bread circles in the remaining berry juices and set a circle on top of each ramekin; the bread should rise above the rims.

Tightly wrap each ramekin in plastic wrap and place on a rimmed baking sheet. Place another rimmed baking sheet on top and weigh down the pan with bags of dried beans or canned goods. Refrigerate the ramekins for at least 8 hours or up to 2 days.

When ready to serve, unwrap the ramekins and invert them onto plates. Pull on the edges of the plastic wrap while twisting off the ramekins. Serve the puddings cold or at room temperature with spoonfuls of crème fraîche.

Brioche is made with milk, eggs, and as much butter as a bread dough can possibly hold, adding luxury to this simple dessert. The bread's fine, cake-like texture soaks up the inky juice of fresh summer blackberries to create a flavorful casing. A spoonful of crème fraîche added just before serving lends an extra measure of richness along with a pleasant tang to offset the intensity of the sweet-tart pudding.

Farm-fresh sweet corn makes the leap from the dinner plate to the ice cream bowl in a surprisingly original dessert. Frosty, creamy corn ice cream, sauced with a fresh blackberry purée, is a delicious celebration of the summer's bounty.

sweet corn ice cream with blackberry sauce

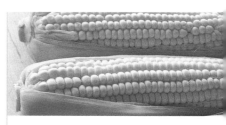

fresh sweet corn, 4 ears

half-and-half, 3 cups

heavy cream, 1 cup, plus
cream as needed

sugar, $\frac{2}{3}$ cup plus $\frac{1}{2}$ cup

salt, pinch

blackberries, $2\frac{1}{2}$ pints

fresh lemon juice,
1 teaspoon

MAKES 1 QUART ICE
CREAM; 6 SERVINGS

Remove the husks and silk from the corn. Using a chef's knife, cut the kernels off the cobs. Add the kernels and cobs to a large pot along with the half-and-half and cream. Add the $\frac{2}{3}$ cup sugar and the salt and bring to a boil over medium-high heat. Reduce the heat to medium-low and simmer, covered, for about 5 minutes, stirring occasionally. Remove from the heat and let steep for at least 3 hours or up to overnight. (If steeping for longer than 3 hours, refrigerate the mixture.)

Strain the corn mixture through a fine-mesh sieve. Using your hands, wring out the cobs and press on the kernels with a spoon to extract as much liquid as possible; discard the cobs and kernels. Measure the liquid; you should have about 3 cups. If not, add more cream as needed. Cover and refrigerate the corn-infused mixture for at least 3 hours or up to 8 hours.

In a nonreactive saucepan, bring the $\frac{1}{2}$ cup sugar and $\frac{1}{4}$ cup water to a boil over medium-high heat. Add 2 pints of the blackberries and stir to combine. Reduce the heat to medium and cook, stirring occasionally, until the berries break down, about 8 minutes. Transfer the mixture to a blender and add the lemon juice. Purée the berry mixture, then it strain through a fine-mesh sieve. Cover and refrigerate until ready to serve.

Freeze the chilled corn-infused mixture in an ice-cream maker according to the manufacturer's directions. If desired, pack it into an airtight container and freeze until very firm.

To serve, scoop the ice cream into bowls, drizzle with the blackberry sauce, top with a few of the remaining blackberries, and serve right away.

The natural sweetness of freshly harvested corn combines with cream to create an unusual——but delicious——ice cream. With a drizzle of fresh blackberry sauce that's a fruity counterpoint to the rich ice cream, this cooling dessert captures summer in a bowl.

raspberry–earl grey tart

Earl Grey tea perfumes this silky tart filling with mysterious hints of citrus and vanilla, and a suggestion of smokiness. The subtle vanilla flavors are echoed in the simple pat-in tart dough and the floral nuances of the fresh raspberries provide an elegant finish.

Using your fingers, press the tart dough into the bottom and up the sides of a 9½-inch fluted tart pan with a removable bottom. Use the bottom of a metal measuring cup dipped in flour to smooth and even out the dough. Press off any excess dough from around the edges of the pan and freeze the tart shell for at least 1 hour or up to 2 days.

Meanwhile, in a small saucepan, bring the cream to a simmer. Remove from the heat, add the tea bags, cover, and let steep for 5 minutes. Gently squeeze the tea bags between 2 spoons to extract as much liquid as possible; discard the tea bags. Transfer the tea-infused cream to a small bowl, cover, and refrigerate until cold, at least 1 hour or up to 2 days.

Preheat the oven to 375°F. Line the frozen tart shell with a large sheet of aluminum foil, letting the edges hang over the sides of the pan. Pour pie weights into the shell. Bake for 25 minutes, lift out the foil and weights, and continue baking until the crust is golden brown, 5–10 minutes longer. Let cool completely on a wire rack.

Pour ¼ cup water into a small saucepan and sprinkle the gelatin over the surface. Set aside for 15 minutes, then warm the mixture over low heat, stirring often, until the gelatin is dissolved, about 2 minutes. Set aside.

In a food processor, combine the chilled tea-infused cream, granulated sugar, crème fraîche, and salt and process until combined. Add the warm gelatin mixture and process until thoroughly combined. Pour the filling into the cooled tart shell and spread it evenly, leaving a slight mound in the center. Arrange the raspberries on top of the filling, loosely cover with plastic wrap, and refrigerate for at least 6 hours or up to overnight.

Remove the tart from its pan and place on a cake plate or platter. Sift confectioners' sugar over the tart, slice, and serve.

vanilla tart dough (page 143)

all-purpose flour

heavy cream, 1 cup

earl grey tea bags, 2

unflavored gelatin, 1 tablespoon (about 2 packets)

granulated sugar, 1 cup

crème fraîche (page 144 or puchased), 1 cup

salt, pinch

raspberries, 3 pints

confectioners' sugar for dusting

MAKES 8 SERVINGS

caramelized nectarines with moscato d'asti zabaglione

nectarines, preferably freestone, 6

honey, 1 tablespoon

nonstick cooking spray

sugar, ½ cup

large egg yolks, 4

moscato d'asti, ⅓ cup

salt, pinch

MAKES 6 SERVINGS

Halve and pit the nectarines, then cut them into ½-inch wedges. Add the wedges to a large bowl, drizzle with the honey, and toss to coat.

Position a rack 3–4 inches from the heating element and preheat the broiler to high. Line a rimmed baking sheet with aluminum foil and lightly spray with nonstick cooking spray.

Pour ¼ cup of the sugar into a bowl and dip one of the cut sides of each nectarine wedge into the sugar. Set the wedges, sugared sides up, on the baking sheet and broil until the sugar is bubbling and the nectarines start to brown, 2–4 minutes; check often as broilers' heat varies. Set aside to cool.

Meawhile, to make the zabaglione, in a saucepan, bring 1½ inches of water to a gentle simmer. In a large stainless-steel bowl, whisk together the egg yolks, *moscato d'Asti*, salt, and remaining ¼ cup sugar. Place the bowl over the saucepan, making sure the bottom does not touch the simmering water. Cook the mixture, whisking constantly, until pale and thick, 6–8 minutes. Remove the bowl from the saucepan.

Divide the nectarines among dessert bowls or plates, top with the zabaglione, and serve right away.

Sparkling moscato d'Asti brings a fruity, honeyed essence to zabaglione, a satiny Italian custard sauce. Here, zabaglione adds richness to tree-ripened nectarines whose texture is softened, flavors are concentrated, and sugars are caramelized under the intense, searing heat of a broiler.

Aromatic five-spice is a ubiquitous seasoning in savory Chinese cooking. Here, its bold, intriguing flavor—warm, peppery, and earthy—is a delicious and unusual accent for juicy, plump summer plums in these charming individual tartlets.

five spice–infused plum tartlets

fresh ginger, one 1-inch piece, peeled and grated

unsalted butter, 3 tablespoons, at room temperature

sugar, 4 tablespoons

all-purpose flour, 1 tablespoon, plus flour for dusting

salt, pinch

chinese five-spice powder, 1 teaspoon

plums, 4

lime, ½

frozen all-butter puff pastry, one 9-by-9½-inch sheet, thawed

MAKES 6 TARTLETS

In a small bowl, stir together the ginger, butter, 3 tablespoons of the sugar, the 1 tablespoon flour, and the salt. Set aside.

In a bowl, mix together the remaining 1 tablespoon sugar and the five-spice powder. Halve and pit the plums, then cut them into ½- to ¾-inch cubes. Add the plums to the bowl with the sugar and five-spice powder. Squeeze the juice from the lime half over the plums and toss well.

Place the puff pastry on a lightly floured work surface and sprinkle the top with flour. Roll the pastry into a 12-by-8-inch rectangle. Cut the rectangle in half lengthwise, then cut each half crosswise into thirds; you should have six 4-inch squares. Brush off any excess flour from the dough. Prick the dough squares all over with a fork, then fit the squares into six 3-inch tartlet pans, pressing the pastry into the bottom and up the sides of the pans. Press off any excess dough hanging over the sides of the pans.

Spread about ½ tablespoon of the ginger-butter mixture over the bottom of each tartlet, then top with the plums, dividing them evenly. Refrigerate the tartlets on a rimmed baking sheet for 30 minutes.

Preheat the oven to 400°F.

Bake the tartlets on the baking sheet for 10 minutes, then reduce the heat to 375°F and continue baking until puffed and browned around the edges, about 10 minutes longer. Let the tartlets cool completely on a wire rack.

Remove the tartlets from their pans and serve on individual plates.

In these tartlets, five-spice infuses sweet-and-sour ripe plums with a warm, exotic flavor and hints of savoriness, while fresh ginger adds a peppery heat. The butter in the filling and pastry shells brings a roundness to the spices, making them taste full and intense.

fall

apple galette with salted caramel

apples, preferably crispin or pink lady, 3

lemon, 1

granulated sugar, 1⅓ cups

ground cinnamon, ½ teaspoon

salt, pinch

all-purpose flour

basic galette dough (page 143)

large egg, 1

turbinado sugar, 2 tablespoons

unsalted butter, 2 tablespoons

heavy cream, ½ cup

dark rum, 3 tablespoons

fleur de sel or coarse sea salt, ½ teaspoon

MAKES 6–8 SERVINGS

Preheat the oven to 400°F. Line a rimmed baking sheet with parchment paper. Peel, halve, core, and cut the apples into ¼-inch slices, then add them to a bowl. Finely grate the zest from the lemon into the bowl, then squeeze 1 tablespoon lemon juice over the apples. Add ⅓ cup of the granulated sugar, the cinnamon, and salt and toss well.

On a lightly floured work surface, roll out the dough into a 15- to 16-inch round about ¼ inch thick. Fold the dough into quarters and unfold it onto the prepared baking sheet. Arrange the apples in the center of the dough, leaving a 3-inch border uncovered. Fold the dough edges over the apples, loosely pleating the dough and leaving the galette open in the center.

In a bowl, whisk the egg with 1 tablespoon water. Brush the dough with the egg mixture and sprinkle with the turbinado sugar. Cut 1 tablespoon of the butter into small pieces and scatter over the apples. Refrigerate the galette for 30 minutes. Bake the galette until the crust is deeply browned, 30–40 minutes. Let cool on the baking sheet on a wire rack.

Meanwhile, in a heavy saucepan, combine the remaining 1 cup granulated sugar and 3 tablespoons water. Cover and bring to a simmer over medium heat, checking the sugar often. Once the sugar starts to melt, uncover and swirl the pan occasionally until the sugar is dissolved, about 5 minutes. Continue to simmer, uncovered, until the sugar turns into a deep amber-brown caramel, 3–5 minutes longer. Remove from the heat, carefully add the cream (the caramel will hiss and bubble vigorously), and whisk until smooth. Whisk in the remaining 1 tablespoon butter, the rum, and *fleur de sel*. Let cool slightly.

To serve, transfer the galette to a platter or cutting board, cut it into wedges, divide among serving plates, and drizzle with the caramel.

A generous measure of sea salt heightens the seductive bittersweetness of the caramel that is drizzled onto this rustic free-form tart just before serving. The result is a full, deep caramel flavor that pairs perfectly with tender lemon-scented apples encased in a buttery, flaky crust.

fresh fig tart with amaretti crust

In this recipe, crushed amaretti cookies bring their almond essence as well as a crispness to a simple press-in tart dough, and anise seeds add hints of licorice. The filling showcases plump, honeyed figs flavored with orange liqueur and fragrant orange zest.

Add the dried figs to a small bowl. Pour the Grand Marnier over the figs and set aside for at least 1 hour or up to overnight.

Position a rack in the lower third of the oven and preheat to 400°F.

In a food processor, combine the 1¼ cups flour, the amaretti cookies, anise seeds, and salt and process until the amaretti are finely ground. Add the butter to the food processor and pulse until the butter pieces are no larger than small peas. Drizzle 4 tablespoons of the ice water over the flour mixture and pulse to combine. Squeeze a small piece of dough; if it doesn't hold together, add 1 more tablespoon of ice water and pulse to combine.

Turn the dough out onto a lightly floured work surface and knead a few times, just until it comes together, then pat into a disk. Dip your fingertips in flour and press the dough into the bottom and up the sides of a 9-inch square fluted tart pan with a removable bottom. Use the bottom of a metal measuring cup dipped in flour to smooth and even out the dough. Press off any excess dough from around the edges of the pan. Prick the bottom of the dough with a fork and bake until just beginning to color, 12–15 minutes. Let cool on a wire rack. Reduce the oven temperature to 375°F.

Combine the dried figs and Grand Marnier, the cream, the ⅓ cup sugar, and the orange zest in a blender and blend until the dried figs are broken into tiny bits. Cut the fresh figs lengthwise into quarters, add them to a bowl, sprinkle with the remaining 1 tablespoon sugar, and toss to coat. Arrange the fresh figs in the tart shell, cut sides up. Place the tart on a rimmed baking sheet and pour the cream mixture over the top.

Bake the tart until the filling jiggles very slightly, about 30 minutes. Let cool completely on a wire rack. Remove the tart from its pan, slice, and serve.

dried figs, preferably sulfite free, 4, chopped

grand marnier, 3 tablespoons

all-purpose flour, 1¼ cups, plus flour as needed

whole amaretti cookies, ¾ cup

anise seeds, 1 teaspoon

salt, ¼ teaspoon

cold unsalted butter, 7 tablespoons, cut into ½-inch pieces

ice water, 4–5 tablespoons

heavy cream, ¾ cup

sugar, ⅓ cup plus 1 tablespoon

orange zest, 1 teaspoon finely grated

fresh black mission figs, ½ pound (about 8 figs)

MAKES 8 SERVINGS

Toasted pecans along with buttermilk and brown sugar add character to a new twist on classic pumpkin pie. With these rich, earthy elements in the crisp crust and creamy filling, this version boasts especially warm, comforting flavors.

brown sugar pumpkin pie with toasted pecan crust

Moist, molasses-rich dark brown sugar and tangy buttermilk add depth to an otherwise traditional pumpkin pie filling. It's baked in a simple cookie-like press-in crust made by grinding smoky toasted pecans and mixing them with butter, flour, and sugar. The result is a comforting dessert full of warmth and earthiness.

Position one rack in the bottom of the oven, another rack in the middle of the oven, and preheat the oven to 350°F.

On a rimmed baking sheet, toast the pecans on the middle rack until fragrant and lightly browned, 5–6 minutes. Pour onto a plate to cool, then finely grind in a food processor; take care not to overprocess them.

In a large bowl, using a wooden spoon, beat the butter and granulated sugar until thoroughly blended. Beat in the egg yolk and flaky sea salt. Add the ground pecans and 1¼ cups flour and stir, working the dry ingredients into the butter mixture by smearing it against the sides of the bowl, until the dough comes together in large, shaggy clumps.

On a lightly floured work surface, press the dough into a mound and knead until it just comes together. Press the dough into a flat disk, then transfer to a 9-inch pie dish. Press the dough evenly into the bottom and up the sides of the dish. Use the bottom of a metal measuring cup dipped in flour to smooth and even out the dough. Crimp the edges with the tines of a fork, then freeze the pie shell for 30 minutes.

Meanwhile, in a food processor, combine the brown sugar, cinnamon, ginger, nutmeg, cloves, and salt and process until smooth. Add the pumpkin purée, buttermilk, and whole eggs and process until combined.

Place the frozen pie shell on a rimmed baking sheet. Pour the filling into the shell and bake on the middle oven rack for 30 minutes. Remove the pie from the baking sheet and transfer directly to the lower oven rack. Bake until the center jiggles only slightly when the pie is tapped, 10–15 minutes longer. Let cool completely on a wire rack.

To serve, cut into wedges and top with whipped cream.

pecan halves, ½ cup

unsalted butter, ½ cup, at room temperature

granulated sugar, ⅓ cup

large egg yolk, 1

flaky sea salt, such as maldon, 1 teaspoon

all-purpose flour, 1¼ cups, plus flour as needed

dark brown sugar, 1 cup firmly packed

ground cinnamon, 2 teaspoons

ground ginger, 2 teaspoons

freshly grated nutmeg, 1 teaspoon

ground cloves, ¼ teaspoon

salt, ½ teaspoon

pumpkin purée, 1 can (15 ounces)

buttermilk, ¾ cup

large eggs, 3

sweetened whipped cream (page 144) for serving

MAKES 8 SERVINGS

spiced pear upside-down cake

unsalted butter, ¾ cup plus 5 tablespoons, at room temperature, plus butter for greasing

light brown sugar, ⅔ cup firmly packed

maple syrup, 2 tablespoons

ripe pears, preferably bartlett or anjou, 2

granulated sugar, ¾ cup plus 1 tablespoon

ground cinnamon, 1 teaspoon

ground cardamom, 1 teaspoon

ground cloves, ¼ teaspoon

all-purpose flour, 1½ cups

baking powder, 2 teaspoons

salt, 1 teaspoon

whole milk, ¾ cup

pure vanilla extract, 2 teaspoons

large eggs, 2

MAKES 8 SERVINGS

Preheat the oven to 350°F. Grease a 9-inch round cake pan with butter.

In a bowl, using a wooden spoon, vigorously beat the 5 tablespoons butter, the brown sugar, and maple syrup until thoroughly blended. Spread this mixture over the bottom of the prepared cake pan.

Peel, halve, and core the pears, and then cut them into ¼-inch slices. Add the pears to a bowl; sprinkle with the 1 tablespoon granulated sugar, the cinnamon, cardamom, and cloves and toss gently to coat. Arrange the pears in the bottom of the pan, fanning and overlapping them slightly, so that the tapered ends point outward; use the small slices to fill any holes.

In a bowl, whisk together the flour, baking powder, and salt. Pour the milk and vanilla into a liquid measuring cup.

Using a stand mixer on medium-high speed, beat the remaining ¾ cup butter with the ¾ cup granulated sugar until light and fluffy, 1–2 minutes. Beat in the eggs, 1 at a time, scraping the sides of the bowl after each addition. Reduce the mixer speed to low and add the dry ingredients in 3 batches, alternately with the milk mixture in 2 batches. Raise the mixer speed to medium-high and beat for 2 minutes to aerate.

Scrape the batter into the cake pan and spread evenly. Bake until a cake tester inserted into the center comes out clean, 60–70 minutes.

Immediately place a large plate, at least 10 inches in diameter, upside down on top of the cake. Carefully invert the cake with the plate, then lift off the pan, gently shaking the pan if necessary to release the cake. Let cool at least 30 minutes, then cut into wedges and serve.

The instense flavor of cloves is best when used in small amounts. In this recipe, just a touch of cloves complements the other more mellow spices as well as the brown sugar and maple syrup. As they bake, the sliced pears release sweet juices that mingle with the aromatic spices and soak into the rich, buttery cake.

Blue cheese, with its bold, salty edge, is usually reserved for savory dishes, but fall's tart, crisp apples suggest a different pairing. Fruity, salty, sweet, and spicy, baked apples filled with blue cheese is a dessert with layers of wonderful flavor.

baked apples with blue cheese, black pepper, and honey

apples, preferably cortland or pippin, 4

honey, ½ cup plus 1 tablespoon

lemon, ½

apple cider, 1 cup

whole cloves, 8

whole star anise, 3

cinnamon sticks, 2

blue cheese, 3 ounces

freshly ground pepper, 1 teaspoon, plus pepper for garnish

heavy cream, ¼ cup

MAKES 4 SERVINGS

Preheat the oven to 350°F.

Cut a 2-inch-wide cone-shaped section from the stem end of each apple. Using a melon baller, scoop out the cores, working your way almost to the bottoms. Using a paring knife, score around the circumference of the lower third of each apple to prevent it from bursting during baking.

Place the apples in an 8-inch square baking dish. Drizzle the ½ cup honey and squeeze the juice from the lemon half over the apples. Pour the cider over and around the apples. Place the cloves, star anise, and cinnamon sticks in the baking dish. Bake the apples until a paring knife easily slips into the centers, 50–60 minutes.

While the apples are baking, crumble the cheese and measure ½ cup lightly packed; save the rest for garnish. In a small bowl, mash together the blue cheese, the 1 tablespoon honey, the pepper, and cream. Remove the apples from the oven and fill the center of each with the blue cheese mixture, dividing it evenly. Let the filled apples cool for 10–15 minutes.

Garnish the apples with a few bits of the reserved crumbled blue cheese and a sprinkle of pepper. Transfer the apples to bowls, drizzle with some of the pan juices, and serve right away.

This new spin on classic baked apples blurs the line between sweet and savory. Piquant blue cheese is the star here; fragrant spices and sweet honey play supporting roles. The apples are filled after baking and their warmth brings together all of the robust sweet-salty flavors.

coconut rice pudding with gingered asian pears

Asian pears taste of a cross between apples and traditional pears, but with fresh hints of pine and a distinct grittiness. Chunks of the crisp fruit, accented by spicy fresh ginger, add a refreshing quality to this rice pudding that is rich and creamy with half-and-half and coconut milk.

In a large saucepan, combine the rice, 3½ cups of the half-and-half, the coconut milk, sugar, and salt and bring to a boil over high heat. Reduce the heat to medium-low, cover, and cook, stirring once or twice, until the rice is tender, 20–30 minutes. Set aside to cool slightly or refrigerate; the rice pudding can be served warm, at room temperature, or cold.

To toast the coconut, preheat the oven to 375°F. Place the coconut on a rimmed baking sheet and bake until fragrant and golden, 6–8 minutes, stirring halfway through baking. Transfer to a small bowl and let cool.

When ready to serve, peel, halve, and core the Asian pears, then cut them into ½-inch cubes. Add the pears to a bowl along with the ginger and brown sugar and toss gently to coat.

Stir the remaining ½ cup half-and-half into the rice pudding. Spoon the pudding into bowls, top with the pears, sprinkle with the toasted coconut flakes, and serve right away.

basmati rice, 1½ cups

half-and-half, 4 cups

unsweetened coconut milk, 1 can (14 ounces)

sugar, 1 cup

salt, pinch

unsweetened coconut flakes, 1½ cups

asian pears, 2

fresh ginger, one 1-inch piece, peeled and grated

light brown sugar, 2 tablespoons firmly packed

MAKES 8 SERVINGS

steamed **persimmon** pudding with **bourbon** whipped cream

unsalted butter,
7 tablespoons, melted, plus
butter for greasing

sugar, 1 cup plus
2 tablespoons

bourbon, 1/3 cup

dried currants, 1/2 cup

all-purpose flour, 1 cup

ground cinnamon,
1 teaspoon

ground cardamom,
1 teaspoon

ground cloves, 1/4 teaspoon

salt, 1/2 teaspoon

orange, 1

baking soda, 2 teaspoons

**ripe, soft hachiya
persimmons,** 3

large egg, 1

pure vanilla extract,
2 teaspoons

**sweetened whipped cream
(page 144)**

MAKES 8 SERVINGS

Place a collapsible steamer insert in a stockpot wide and tall enough to fit a 1½-quart fluted pudding mold. Fill the pot with enough water to reach the bottom of the steamer. Generously grease the inside of the pudding mold with butter. Sprinkle the bottom and sides with the 2 tablespoons sugar and shake the mold to coat evenly. Tap out the excess sugar.

In a small saucepan, bring the bourbon to a simmer. Add the currants, cover, and remove from the heat. In a bowl, whisk together the flour, cinnamon, cardamom, cloves, and salt.

Finely grate the zest from the orange and add it to a food processor along with the 1 cup sugar. Squeeze 2 tablespoons orange juice into a small bowl. Stir in the baking soda and set aside. Process the sugar and orange zest until the sugar is fragrant and tinted orange, 10–15 seconds. Halve the persimmons, remove any large seeds, and scoop the pulp into the processor. Add the egg and vanilla, process until smooth, then add the orange-juice mixture and process to combine. Transfer the mixture to a large bowl and whisk in the flour-spice mixture.

Place the stockpot on the stove top and bring the water to a boil over high heat. Strain the currants, reserving the bourbon, and whisk them into the batter along with the melted butter. Transfer the batter to the prepared mold, snap on the cover, and place the mold on the steamer insert. Reduce the heat so the water is at a simmer and cover the pot. Cook until a cake tester inserted into the pudding comes out clean, 1½–1¾ hours. Remove the mold from the pot and let cool for 10 minutes, then invert the pudding onto a platter and let cool completely.

To serve, whisk 2–3 tablespoons of the reserved bourbon into the whipped cream. Slice the pudding and serve with the bourbon whipped cream.

The creamy, custardy pulp of fully ripe Hachiya persimmons is honey-sweet and has an earthy, slightly savory quality. In this moist, cake-like pudding, persimmons and fragrant, warm spices come together to create a rich, comforting dessert.

poached quince with mascarpone, caramel, and gingersnaps

Thick, rich, mascarpone tastes of fresh cream with a subtle butteriness. It pairs perfectly with apple-and-pear-like quince, whose delicate floral aroma is brought out by gentle poaching in spiced Riesling wine. A drizzle of caramel lends a bittersweet flavor and crushed gingersnaps add texture to this simple, but very elegant, dessert.

Pour the Riesling into a deep nonreactive saucepan. Add 1 cup of the sugar, the cinnamon sticks, star anise, and peppercorns and bring to a simmer over medium-high heat.

Peel and halve the quinces. Add the quince halves to the simmering wine, return to a simmer, then reduce the heat to medium-low. Cover and cook until a paring knife easily slips into the quinces, about 1 hour (the cores will remain slightly hard). Let the quinces cool in the poaching liquid.

In a heavy saucepan, combine the remaining 1 cup sugar and 3 tablespoons water. Cover and bring to a simmer over medium-high heat, checking the sugar often. Once the sugar starts to melt, uncover and swirl the pan occasionally until the sugar is dissolved, about 5 minutes. Continue to simmer, uncovered, until the sugar turns into a deep amber-brown caramel, 3–5 minutes longer. Remove from the heat, carefully add the cream (the caramel will hiss and bubble vigorously), and whisk until smooth. Whisk in the butter, vanilla, and salt. Let cool slightly.

In a bowl, whisk the mascarpone to soften, then whisk in 3 tablespoons of the cooled poaching liquid. Using a rolling pin, crush the gingersnaps into small pieces (you should have about ½ cup). Using a melon baller, core the poached quince halves and place each half on a serving plate or in a bowl. Top the quince halves with the mascarpone mixture, drizzle with the caramel, sprinkle with the crushed gingersnaps, and serve.

riesling wine, one 750-ml bottle

sugar, 2 cups

cinnamon sticks, 2

whole star anise, 1

black peppercorns, ½ teaspoon

quinces, 3

heavy cream, ⅔ cup

unsalted butter, 3 tablespoons

pure vanilla extract, ½ teaspoon

salt, ¼ teaspoon

mascarpone cheese, ½ pound

gingersnaps, 10–15 two-inch cookies

MAKES 6 SERVINGS

In a simple, modern dessert, roasting renders firm pears sweet and tender and intensifies their delicate bouquet. Fresh bay leaves, usually a seasoning for braises and stews, lend gentle herbal nuances. Golden honey draws out a floral flavor.

roasted pears with honey, bay, and greek yogurt

Fresh bay leaves contain unique hints of pine and white pepper. In this recipe, they lend their intriguing aroma, usually reserved for savory dishes, to a simple dessert of honeyed pears flavored with almond-scented amaretto, toasty nuts, and tart Greek-style yogurt.

Preheat the oven to 375°F. Place the almonds on a rimmed baking sheet and toast in the oven until fragrant and lightly browned, 5–6 minutes. Pour onto a plate to cool. Leave the oven on.

Halve the pears lengthwise. Cut out the fibrous sections connecting the stems to the cores, and then trim off the stems. Using a melon baller, scoop out the cores.

In a Dutch oven, combine the honey and bay leaves and bring to a simmer over medium-high heat. Reduce the heat to medium and continue to simmer, stirring occasionally, until the honey is fragrant and turns a rich amber color, about 3 minutes. Remove from the heat.

Place the butter pieces in the pot with the honey, spacing them evenly. Using tongs, carefully place a pear half, cut side down, on top of each piece of butter. Cover the pot and roast the pears in the oven for 10 minutes. Using a long-handled spoon, gently turn the pears over and baste with the honey mixture. Drizzle the pears with the amaretto and continue to roast, uncovered, until golden brown and a paring knife slips easily into the centers, 6–8 minutes. Remove from the oven and let the pears cool slightly in the honey mixture, about 30 minutes.

In a bowl, whisk the yogurt until smooth. To serve, place each pear half in a bowl, dollop with yogurt, and sprinkle with the toasted almonds. Drizzle with some of the honey mixture from the pot and serve right away.

sliced almonds, 1/3 cup

firm bosc pears, 3

honey, 1/3 cup

fresh bay leaves, 4

unsalted butter,
3 tablespoons, cut into 6 pieces

amaretto, 2 tablespoons

greek-style plain yogurt,
1 1/2 cups

MAKES 6 SERVNGS

dark chocolate and toasted walnut tart

walnut halves, 1½ cups, very coarsely chopped

unsalted butter, ½ cup plus 3 tablespoons, at room temperature

granulated sugar, ⅓ cup

large egg yolk, 1

flaky sea salt, such as maldon, 1 teaspoon

all-purpose flour, 1¼ cups, plus flour as needed

corn syrup, ½ cup

large eggs, 2

light brown sugar, 3 tablespoons firmly packed

pure vanilla extract, ¾ teaspoon

salt, ⅛ teaspoon

bittersweet chocolate, ¼ pound, finely chopped

MAKES 10 SERVINGS

Place one rack in the bottom of the oven, another rack in the lower third of the oven, and preheat the oven to 375°F.

On a rimmed baking sheet, toast the walnuts on the upper oven rack until fragrant, 6–8 minutes. Pour onto a plate to cool. Finely grind ⅓ cup of the chopped walnuts in the food processor; take care not to overprocess them.

In a bowl, using a wooden spoon, beat the ½ cup butter and the granulated sugar until thoroughly blended. Beat in the egg yolk and flaky sea salt. Add the ground walnuts and 1¼ cups flour and stir, working the dry ingredients into the butter mixture by smearing it against the sides of the bowl, until the dough comes together in large, shaggy clumps.

On a lightly floured work surface, press the dough into a mound and knead until it just comes together. Press the dough into a rectangle, then transfer it to a 13-by-4-inch fluted rectangular tart pan with a removable bottom. Press the dough evenly into the bottom and up the sides of the pan. Press off any excess dough from the edges of the pan. Place the tart shell on a rimmed baking sheet and bake on the lower rack until lightly browned, about 12 minutes. Remove from the oven and use a fork to gently press down the bottom of the shell if it has puffed up during baking.

In a bowl, combine the corn syrup, eggs, brown sugar, vanilla, and salt. Melt the remaining 3 tablespoons butter, then whisk into the corn-syrup mixture. Stir the chopped chocolate into the mixture along with the reserved walnuts. Pour the filling into the crust and bake on the upper oven rack until the center of the tart is puffed and set, about 25 minutes. Let cool completely on a wire rack.

To serve, remove the tart from its pan and cut into slices.

This midly sweet tart is loaded with pleasantly bitter walnuts both inside and out. Toasting the walnuts coaxes out their nutty flavor and crisps their texture. The dark chocolate in the filling adds yet another element of bitterness that is tempered by fragrant vanilla and the richness of butter and eggs.

In the cooking of southern France, lavender is used to season hearty meats and roasts, but its distinct taste is also wonderful in desserts. It brings a sweet, floral quality to creamy egg-rich custards, and an unexpected undercurrent of herbal flavor.

lavender crème brûlée

heavy cream, 2½ cups

sugar, ½ cup plus
2 tablespoons

salt, pinch

dried lavender, 2 teaspoons

large egg yolks, 8

MAKES 6 SERVINGS

Preheat the oven to 325°F. In a saucepan, combine the cream, the ½ cup sugar, and the salt and bring to a boil, stirring occasionally. Remove from the heat, stir in the lavender, cover, and let stand for 15 minutes.

In a large bowl, whisk the egg yolks to combine. A little at a time, begin whisking the warm cream into the yolks until the bottom of the bowl is warm. Whisk in the remaining cream a little more quickly. Pour through a fine-mesh sieve into a large liquid measuring cup; discard the lavender.

Place six ¾-cup ramekins in a 13-by-9-by-2-inch baking dish. Divide the egg yolk–cream mixture evenly among the ramekins. Transfer the dish to the oven and pour enough very hot water into the dish to come halfway up the sides of the ramekins. Bake until the custards jiggle just slightly in the centers when the ramekins are gently shaken, 30–35 minutes. Carefully remove the baking dish from the oven and let the custards cool in the water bath for 30 minutes. Remove the ramekins from the the baking dish, wipe the bottoms dry, and wrap each in plastic wrap. Refrigerate for at least 4 hours or up to 3 days.

Unwrap the custards and gently blot the tops with a paper towel to soak up any moisture on the surface. Sprinkle the 2 tablespoons sugar over the tops of the custards, dividing evenly; tilt and tap each ramekin to distribute the sugar evenly on the custard's surface. Using a handheld kitchen torch, caramelize the sugar by moving the torch in a figure-eight motion until the sugar is evenly browned and melted. (Alternatively, place an oven rack 3–4 inches below the heating element and preheat the broiler. Place the ramekins on a rimmed baking sheet and broil until the sugar bubbles and caramelizes, 1–2 minutes.) Serve right away.

Dried lavender blossoms add their perfume to these perfectly smooth custards. Lavender's floral, slightly herbal quality offsets the richness of the egg yolks and heavy cream and its savory nuances intensify the bittersweet taste of the crackly sugar crust.

winter

olive oil–madeira cake with blood orange compote

unsalted butter

sugar, 1⅓ cups plus
6 tablespoons

cake flour, 3 cups

baking powder,
2½ teaspoons

salt, ¾ teaspoon

large eggs, 3

orange zest, 1 teaspoon
finely grated

pure vanilla extract,
½ teaspoon

**medium-sweet or sweet
madeira,** ⅔ cup

whole milk, ½ cup

extra-virgin olive oil, ¾ cup

blood oranges, 4

pomegranate juice, ⅓ cup

fresh mint leaves, 10, finely
chopped

orange marmalade, 1 cup

MAKES 12 SERVINGS

Preheat the oven to 350°F. Generously grease a one-piece tube pan with butter, then sprinkle the bottom and sides with 2 tablespoons of the sugar, tilting and tapping the pan to coat it evenly.

In a bowl, whisk together the flour, baking powder, and salt. Using a stand mixer on high speed, beat the eggs, orange zest, vanilla, and the 1⅓ cups sugar until thick and pale, about 3 minutes. With the mixer running, add the Madeira and milk in a slow, steady stream, then drizzle in the olive oil and beat until thoroughly blended. Stop the mixer and sift the dry ingredients over the egg mixture in 3 batches, folding it in with a rubber spatula until only a few dry streaks remain.

Scrape the batter into the prepared pan. Bake until the cake is browned and a cake tester inserted into the center comes out clean, 45–50 minutes. Let cool to room temperature in the pan on a wire rack, about 2 hours.

Meanwhile, using a paring knife, cut away the peel from the blood oranges and cut the flesh into segments (page 147), reserving any juice. In a nonreactive saucepan, bring the pomegranate juice and remaining 4 tablespoons sugar to a simmer over medium-high heat. Simmer, stirring occasionally, until the mixture is reduced by half, 4–6 minutes. Add the blood orange segments and juice and return to a simmer. Reduce the heat to medium-low and continue to simmer until the orange segments have broken down, 5–8 minutes. Stir in the mint and orange marmalade. Transfer the compote to a bowl and let cool to room temperature.

To serve, invert the cake onto a large plate, then turn it right side up. Cut the cake into wedges, divide among serving plates, and top with the blood orange compote.

Fruity extra-virgin olive oil replaces butter in this unique cake. The batter is scented with fresh orange zest along with sweet, raisiny Madeira. The cake's orange flavor is amplified by a compote of blood oranges and orange marmalade, with chopped fresh mint stirred in for a cooling touch.

banana-raisin bread pudding with brandy sauce

The familiar taste of ripe bananas brings a new twist to a classic bread pudding that is also accented by fragrant vanilla, full-flavored brown sugar, and a silky brandy sauce. Starting with cinnamon-raisin bread instead of a plain loaf is a simple way to add dimension to this rich, comforting dessert.

Preheat the oven to 350°F. Place the bread on a rimmed baking sheet and bake the squares until the bread is dry, 6–8 minutes. Reduce the oven heat to 325°F. Grease a 3-quart baking dish with the room-temperature butter.

In a large bowl, whisk together 3 cups of the cream, the milk, 3 of the egg yolks, the whole eggs, the ⅔ cup granulated sugar, the vanilla, and salt. Submerge the dried bread in the mixture and let soak for 30 minutes, stirring and pressing the bread into the liquid every 10 minutes.

Peel the bananas, cut them lengthwise into quarters, and then crosswise into ¼-inch slices. Add to a bowl with the brown sugar and toss well.

Place half of the soaked bread in the prepared baking dish and cover evenly with the bananas. Top with the remaining bread, pour any remaining cream-egg mixture over the top, drizzle with the melted butter, and sprinkle with about 1 tablespoon granulated sugar.

Place the baking dish in a large roasting pan, transfer the pan to the oven, and pour 1 inch of very hot water into the roasting pan. Bake until the top is golden brown and the pudding is just set, about 1 hour. Let cool in the water bath on a wire rack.

Meanwhile, in a saucepan, whisk together the remaining 1¾ cups cream, the remaining 4 egg yolks, and the ½ cup granulated sugar. Cook over medium-low heat, whisking constantly, until the mixture is thick enough to coat the back of a wooden spoon, 5–6 minutes (do not let the mixture boil). Whisk in the brandy, then strain through a fine-mesh sieve.

To serve, spoon the warm pudding into bowls and drizzle with the sauce.

sliced cinnamon-raisin bread, 1½ pounds, cut into 1-inch squares

unsalted butter, 2 tablespoons, at room temperature, plus 2 tablespoons, melted

heavy cream, 4¾ cups

whole milk, 3 cups

large egg yolks, 7

large eggs, 3

granulated sugar, ⅔ cup plus ½ cup, plus sugar for sprinkling

pure vanilla extract, 1 teaspoon

salt, ¼ teaspoon

ripe bananas, 4

dark brown sugar, 2 tablespoons firmly packed

brandy, 3 tablespoons

MAKES 12 SERVINGS

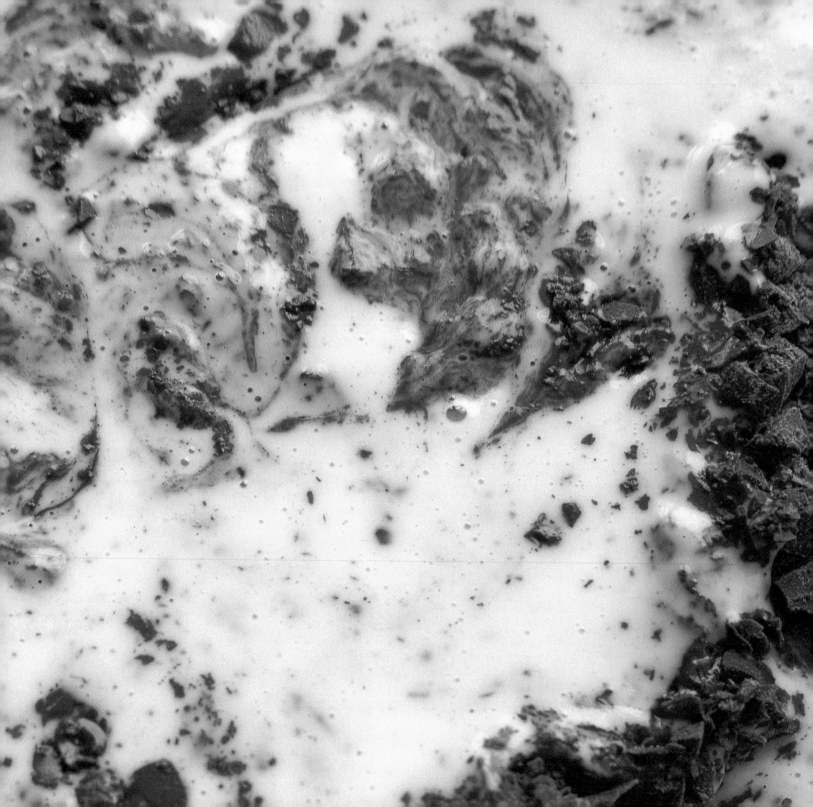

Winter's colorful tangerines are an unexpected accent for a creamy pudding-like custard made with bittersweet chocolate and luxurious heavy cream. Together, they create a rich dessert that is perfectly balanced by fresh, lively citrus flavor.

chocolate-tangerine
pots de crème

Tangerines lend their distinct taste to this rich custard dessert. Their bright, fragrant zest perfumes an intense dark-chocolate custard, while the tangy juice perks up a vanilla mixture. The two are swirled together to create a wonderful contrast in color as well as complementary tastes.

Finely grate the zest from the tangerines, then squeeze 3 tablespoons tangerine juice. Place the chocolate in a heatproof bowl.

In a saucepan, whisk together the egg yolks, sugar, vanilla, salt, and tangerine zest. Whisk the cream into the egg mixture, then cook over medium heat, whisking constantly, until the mixture is thick enough to coat the back of a wooden spoon (do not let the mixture boil). Strain the mixture through a fine-mesh sieve into a large bowl. Pour two-thirds of the hot mixture over the chocolate, let sit for 5 minutes, then whisk to combine. Whisk the tangerine juice into the remaining plain mixture.

Using a small ladle, fill six ¾-cup ramekins one-third full with the chocolate mixture. Pour the tangerine mixture into the ramekins, dividing it evenly, then top with the remaining chocolate mixture. Drag a toothpick or skewer through the mixtures in the ramekins, swirling in a figure-eight motion, to create a marbled effect. Cover with plastic wrap and refrigerate for at least 2 hours or up to 3 days. Serve the pots de crème chilled.

tangerines, 2

bittersweet chocolate, 6 ounces, chopped

large egg yolks, 6

sugar, ⅓ cup

pure vanilla extract, 1 teaspoon

salt, ¼ teaspoon

heavy cream, 2½ cups

MAKES 6 SERVINGS

meyer lemon mousse with graham cracker crumble

graham crackers, 6 ounces (1 sleeve from a 14-ounce box)

sugar, 1⅔ cups plus 3 tablespoons

salt

unsalted butter, ½ cup, melted, plus 6 tablespoons

meyer lemons, 5

large eggs, 5, at room temperature

heavy cream, 1½ cups

ricotta cheese, ¾ cup, at room temperature

MAKES 6 SERVINGS

Preheat the oven to 325°F. Line a rimmed baking sheet with aluminum foil.

Add the graham crackers to a food processor, pulse to break them up a bit, and then process into fine crumbs. Add the 3 tablespoons sugar, a pinch of salt, and the melted butter and pulse until the mixture comes together in small nuggets. Transfer to the prepared baking sheet and bake until light golden brown, about 10 minutes. Let cool to room temperature.

Finely grate 1 tablespoon zest from the Meyer lemons, then squeeze 1 cup Meyer lemon juice. Add the zest and juice to a nonreactive saucepan. Whisk in the eggs, 1⅓ cups of the sugar, and a pinch of salt. Cook the mixture over medium-low heat, whisking constantly, until it thickens and turns bright yellow, 4–5 minutes (do not let the mixture boil). Remove from the heat, whisk in the 6 tablespoons butter, and then strain the curd through a fine-mesh sieve into a bowl. Set aside to cool for 15 minutes, then cover with plastic wrap, pressing it directly onto the surface of the curd. Refrigerate until cold, at least 1½ hours.

Using a stand mixer, beat the cream and the remaining ⅓ cup sugar until the cream holds firm peaks. Add the chilled lemon curd and the ricotta and beat until smooth, scraping the sides of the bowl as needed.

When ready to serve, spoon half of the mousse into the bottom of each of 6 parfait glasses, dividing it evenly. Sprinkle with half of the graham cracker crumble, again dividing evenly. Repeat the layering with the remaining mousse and graham cracker crumble and serve right away.

Juicy and mildly tart, Meyer lemons have a deep yellow color and fragrant skins. Their juice and zest give this mousse a fresh, bright flavor while ricotta cheese lends it substance and body. Buttered and sugared graham cracker crumbs layered into the mousse and sprinkled on top add sweetness and a crisp contrast in texture.

Fresh rosemary is
so intense that it
is usually used only
in savory dishes.
But here, it gives
buttery pound
cakes a delightful
woodsy fragrance.
Dried fruits soaked
in spice-infused
Port make a bold-
flavored compote
to stand up to the
assertiveness of
the rosemary.

rosemary pound cakes with port-soaked dried fruits

mixed dried fruits, such as cranberries, figs, and apricots, 2 cups

juniper berries, 8

black peppercorns, 1 teaspoon

port, 1 cup

sugar, 1⅔ cups

cinnamon sticks, 2

nonstick cooking spray

unsalted butter, 1 cup

fresh rosemary, 4 small sprigs

cake flour, 1¼ cups

baking powder, ¼ teaspoon

salt, ½ teaspoon

large eggs, 3, at room temperature

large egg yolks, 3, at room temperature

pure vanilla extract, ½ teaspoon

MAKES 8 OR 9 SERVINGS

Cut any large dried fruits into bite-sized pieces. Enclose the juniper berries and peppercorns in a tea ball and place in a saucepan. Add the Port, ⅔ cup of the sugar, and the cinnamon sticks and bring to a simmer, stirring occasionally. Add the dried fruits and simmer for 5 minutes. Remove from the heat, cover, and set aside for at least 1 hour.

Preheat the oven to 350°F. Spray three 5¾-by-3⅛-inch miniature loaf pans with nonstick cooking spray.

Melt the butter in a small saucepan over medium-low heat. Remove from the heat, add 3 rosemary sprigs, cover, and let stand for 15 minutes. Strain through a fine-mesh sieve; discard the rosemary.

While the rosemary steeps, pluck the leaves from the remaining rosemary sprig and coarsely chop the leaves. In a bowl, whisk together the flour, baking powder, salt, and chopped rosemary.

Using a stand mixer on medium-high speed, beat the whole eggs, egg yolks, and vanilla until combined. Add the remaining 1 cup sugar and beat until pale and thick, about 3 minutes. Reduce the speed to low and add the dry ingredients in 2 batches, mixing only until a few dry streaks remain. Raise the mixer speed to medium-low and drizzle in the rosemary-infused butter. Increase the speed to medium and beat until combined. Scrape the batter into the prepared loaf pans, dividing it evenly.

Bake the cakes until domed, brown around the edges, and a cake tester inserted into the centers comes out clean, about 40 minutes. Let cool in the pans for 5 minutes, then invert the cakes onto a wire rack, turn them right sides up, and let cool completely.

To serve, slice the pound cakes and serve with the Port-soaked dried fruits.

Fresh rosemary, with its woodsy character and resinous hints, gives these miniature pound cakes a decidedly savory edge. A hearty compote of spice-infused Port and chunky dried fruits is full of concentrated flavors that perfectly match the bold taste of the pound cakes.

orange crème caramel

Just a modest amount of delicately perfumed orange-flower water gives these silky custards with caramel a refined taste and an air of distinction.

Orange liqueur and a garnish of candied citrus zest provide additional layers of citrus flavor and lend depth to the dessert.

Preheat the oven to 325°F.

In a heavy saucepan, combine 1½ cups of the sugar and ½ cup water. Cover and bring to a simmer over medium-high heat, checking the sugar often. Once the sugar starts to melt, uncover and swirl the pan occasionally until the sugar is dissolved, about 5 minutes. Continue to simmer, uncovered, until the sugar turns into a deep amber-brown caramel, 4–6 minutes longer. Pour the caramel into six ¾-cup ramekins, dividing it evenly. Wearing an oven mitt, carefully tilt the ramekins to coat the sides with caramel. Place the ramekins in a 13-by-9-by-2-inch baking dish.

In a large bowl, whisk together the remaining ½ cup sugar, the egg yolks, whole egg, Grand Marnier, orange-flower water, and salt. In a saucepan, combine the cream and milk and bring to a simmer over medium-high heat. A little at a time, begin whisking the warm cream-milk mixture into the egg mixture until the bottom of the bowl is warm. Whisk in the remaining liquid a little more quickly.

Ladle the egg-cream mixture into the ramekins, dividing it evenly. Transfer the baking dish to the oven and pour enough very hot water into the dish to come halfway up the sides of the ramekins. Bake until the custards jiggle just slightly in the centers when they're gently shaken, about 35 minutes. Carefully remove the baking dish from the oven and let the custards cool in the water bath for 30 minutes. Remove the ramekins from the water bath, wipe the bottoms dry, and wrap each in plastic wrap. Refrigerate for at least 6 hours or up to 3 days.

To serve, unwrap the custards and run a knife around the edges of the ramekins to loosen them. Invert the custards onto plates, lift off the ramekins, garnish with the candied citrus zest, and serve.

sugar, 2 cups

large egg yolks, 4

large egg, 1

grand marnier, 2 tablespoons

orange-flower water, 2 teaspoons

salt, pinch

heavy cream, 1¾ cups

whole milk, ¾ cup

candied citrus zest (page 144) for garnish

MAKES 6 SERVINGS

spicy gingerbread with sherry–cream cheese frosting

unsalted butter, ½ cup, melted, plus butter for greasing

all-purpose flour, 2 cups

ground ginger, 1 tablespoon

ground cinnamon, 1½ teaspoons

ground cloves, ½ teaspoon

finely ground black pepper, ½ teaspoon

cayenne pepper, ⅛ teaspoon

salt, ¾ teaspoon

baking powder and baking soda, ½ teaspoon *each*

large eggs, 2

light brown sugar, 1 cup firmly packed

dark molasses, ⅔ cup

whole milk, 1 cup

fresh ginger, one 4-inch piece, peeled and grated

sherry–cream cheese frosting (page 144)

MAKES 9 SERVINGS

Preheat the oven to 350°F. Grease an 8-inch square baking dish with butter.

In a bowl, whisk together the flour, ground ginger, cinnamon, cloves, black pepper, cayenne pepper, salt, baking powder, and baking soda.

In another bowl, whisk the eggs, then add the brown sugar and whisk vigorously to combine. Whisk in the molasses and milk. Add the grated fresh ginger and whisk well.

Pour the egg mixture into the bowl with the flour mixture and stir with a rubber spatula a few times to moisten the ingredients. While stirring, drizzle in the melted butter, mixing just until blended.

Scrape the batter into the prepared baking dish and spread it evenly. Bake until the center springs back when pressed lightly with a fingertip and a cake tester inserted into the center comes out clean, about 40 minutes. Let cool to room temperature in the pan on a wire rack.

Using an icing spatula, spread the frosting to the cooled cake. Cut the frosted cake into 9 squares and serve.

Fragrant spices give this gingerbread big, bold character. Among them is fiery red cayenne pepper that adds an undercurrent of heat and leaves a lingering flavor on the palate. The rich cream cheese frosting lends a welcome tanginess that balances the spiciness of the velvety cake.

Ruby-red fresh cranberries form a festive and flavorful crown on a holiday Bundt cake. Their assertive tartness is tempered by a generous measure of sugar baked into the cake, as well as by a final flourish of sweet lemon glaze on top.

glazed cranberry-lemon cake

unsalted butter, ¾ cup, at room temperature, plus butter for greasing

light brown sugar, ⅓ cup firmly packed

fresh cranberries, 3 cups (about 12 ounces)

all-purpose flour, 2½ cups

baking powder, 2½ teaspoons

baking soda, ½ teaspoon

salt, 1 teaspoon

granulated sugar, 1½ cups

lemons, 2

buttermilk, ¾ cup

pure vanilla extract, 1½ teaspoons

large eggs, 3

confectioners' sugar, 1 cup, plus sugar as needed

MAKES 12 SERVINGS

Preheat the oven to 350°F. Generously grease a 12-cup Bundt pan with butter. Sprinkle the brown sugar in the bottom of the pan, then evenly distribute the cranberries over the sugar.

In a bowl, whisk together the flour, baking powder, baking soda, and salt. Add the granulated sugar to the bowl of a stand mixer. Finely grate the zest from the lemons over the sugar and mix briefly.

Squeeze the juice from the lemons. In a liquid measuring cup, combine 2 tablespoons of the lemon juice, the buttermilk, and vanilla; reserve the remaining lemon juice.

Add the ¾ cup butter to the lemon zest–sugar mixture and beat on medium-high speed until light and fluffy, 1–2 minutes. Beat in the eggs, 1 at a time, scraping the sides of the bowl after each addition. Reduce the mixer speed to low and add the dry ingredients in 3 batches, alternating with the buttermilk mixture in 2 batches. Raise the mixer speed to medium-high and beat for 2 minutes to aerate.

Scrape the batter into the pan and spread it evenly over the cranberries. Bake until the cake is browned and a cake tester inserted into the center comes out clean, 35–40 minutes. Let cool in the pan for 5 minutes, then invert the cake onto a cake plate, lift off the pan, and let cool completely.

Once the cake is cool, in a bowl, whisk together the confectioners' sugar and 1½ tablespoons of the reserved lemon juice until thick and smooth. Test the consistency by drizzling a bit of glaze over the cake. If it runs off the cake, whisk in a little more confectioners' sugar; if it sits on the cake without moving, whisk in a little more lemon juice. Drizzle the glaze over cake and let set for at least 15 minutes. Slice into wedges and serve.

Fresh cranberries and bold, bright lemon zest and juice add refreshing qualities to this butter-rich cake. As the cake bakes, the cranberries are transformed into a sweet-tart compote-like topping. A simple lemon glaze is the finishing touch for this delightful dessert.

grapefruit-champagne sorbet

The bittersweet juice of fresh grapefruit and its fragrant zest combine with bubbly, bright-tasting champagne to create this beautiful, pale-pink sorbet. Cool and mildly sweet, it is a refreshing conclusion to an opulent winter meal.

In a blender, combine 2 cups cold water, the champagne, and sugar. Finely grate the zest from 1 of the grapefruits, then squeeze ½ cup grapefruit juice from the zested fruit. Add the grapefruit zest and juice to the blender.

Using a paring knife, cut away the peel from the remaining grapefruit and cut the flesh into segments (page 147), reserving any juice. Squeeze the membrane that's left behind over the blender to extract any additional juice, then discard. Add the grapefruit segments and juices to the blender. Purée until smooth, then pour the mixture into a nonreactive bowl, cover, and refrigerate for 2–3 hours.

Freeze the chilled grapefruit mixture in an ice-cream maker according to the manufacturer's directions. If desired, pack it into an airtight container and freeze until very firm.

Scoop the sorbet into bowls and serve right away.

rosé champagne or sparkling wine, 1 cup

superfine sugar, 1¼ cups

ruby red or pink grapefruit, 2 large

MAKES 1 QUART SORBET;
6–8 SERVINGS

bittersweet chocolate and dark caramel tartlets

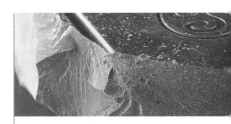

granulated sugar, 1 cup

heavy cream, ⅔ cup plus ¾ cup

unsalted butter, 3 tablespoons

salt, ¼ teaspoon

cocoa tartlet dough (page 142), at room temperature

unsweetened cocoa powder

bittersweet chocolate, 6 ounces, finely chopped

flaky sea salt, such as maldon, ½ teaspoon

MAKES 6 SERVINGS

In a heavy saucepan, combine the sugar and 3 tablespoons water. Cover and bring to a simmer over medium-high heat, checking the sugar often. Once the sugar starts to melt, uncover and swirl the pan occasionally until the sugar is dissolved, about 5 minutes. Continue to simmer, uncovered, until the sugar turns into a very deep amber-brown caramel and has a faint burnt smell, 4–6 minutes longer. Remove from the heat, carefully add the ⅔ cup cream (the caramel will hiss and bubble vigorously), and whisk until smooth. Whisk in the butter and salt and let cool to room temperature.

Preheat the oven to 375°F. Pat the dough into a 6-by-9-inch rectangle. Cut the rectangle in half lengthwise, then cut each half crosswise into thirds; you should have six 3-inch squares. Place each square in a 3-inch tartlet pan, then dip your fingertips in cocoa powder and press the dough into the bottom and up the sides of the pans. Press off any excess dough from around the edges of the pans, and use any scraps to fill cracks or holes. Place the tartlet shells on a rimmed baking sheet and bake until set, about 10 minutes. Let the shells cool on the baking sheet on a wire rack.

Meanwhile, add the chocolate to a small heatproof bowl. In a small saucepan, bring the ¾ cup cream to a simmer and pour over the chocolate. Let stand for 5 minutes, then whisk until smooth.

Fill each tartlet shell with about 1 tablespoon of the caramel, spreading it evenly with the back of a spoon. Pour the chocolate filling into the shells, dividing it evenly and smoothing the tops. Refrigerate until firm, at least 2 hours or up to 2 days, covering with plastic wrap once the chocolate is set.

When ready to serve, let the tartlets stand at room temperature for about 15 minutes to soften slightly. Remove the tartlets from their pans, sprinkle each with a little flaky sea salt, and serve.

In these individual tartlets, the double dose of dark chocolate, from the cocoa crusts and the rich ganache filling, is complemented by an especially toasty and pleasantly bitter dark caramel. A sprinkle of briny sea salt over the tartlets intensifies the flavors and adds a welcome crunch.

Creamy fresh goat cheese goes from cheese plate to cheesecake to make a delicious winter dessert. The silky, tart lemon curd that cloaks the top of the cake echoes the tangy flavor of the filling and counters the rich, lush quality of the cheesecake.

goat cheese–lemon cheesecake

almond biscotti, 6 ounces, broken into pieces

sugar, 1 cup plus 2 tablespoons

unsalted butter, 4 tablespoons, melted

salt

large eggs, 4, at room temperature

pure vanilla extract, ½ teaspoon

lemon oil, ½ teaspoon

neufchâtel cheese, 1 pound, at room temperature

fresh goat cheese, ½ pound, at room temperature

sour cream, 1 cup

lemon curd (page 143)

MAKES 10–12 SERVINGS

Preheat the oven to 325°F. In a food processor, finely grind the biscotti. Add the 2 tablespoons sugar, melted butter, and a pinch of salt and pulse until the mixture resembles wet sand. Transfer to a 9-inch springform pan and press into the bottom and halfway up the sides of the pan. Bake the crust until lightly golden, 10–12 minutes. Let cool, then wrap the outside of the pan with a large sheet of aluminum foil.

In a liquid measuring cup, whisk together the eggs, vanilla, and lemon oil. Using a stand mixer on medium-high speed, beat the Neufchâtel and goat cheeses until light and creamy, about 4 minutes. Beat in the remaining 1 cup sugar and ¼ teaspoon salt until thoroughly blended, 1–2 minutes. Slowly pour in the egg mixture, beating constantly and scraping the sides of the bowl as needed. Add the sour cream and continue beating until the mixture is light and fluffy, about 1 minute longer. Using a rubber spatula, give the mixture a final stir, scraping the sides and bottom of the bowl.

Pour the filling into the crust and spread it evenly. Place the pan in a large roasting pan. Transfer the roasting pan to the oven and pour in 1 inch of very hot water. Bake the cheesecake until just set and a cake tester inserted into the center comes out clean, 1–1¼ hours. (Check after 30 minutes and add more hot water to the pan if needed.) Let the cheesecake cool in the water bath on a wire rack for 1 hour. Remove the aluminum foil, then cover the cheesecake with plastic wrap and refrigerate for at least 1 hour. Spread the lemon curd on the cheesecake. Cover with plastic wrap and refrigerate for at least 2 hours or up to 2 days.

Drench a kitchen towel in hot water, wring well, and wrap it around the springform pan for 10 seconds. Unclasp and remove the pan sides, transfer the cheesecake to a cake plate, slice, and serve.

Goat cheese and lemon partner to create a new take on classic cheesecake. The goat cheese adds a tangy, salty touch and a wonderfully complex flavor; a tart lemon curd topping adds a freshness that offsets the richness of the cheesecake. A crumb crust made with almond biscotti brings a subtle nuttiness and crisp texture to the dessert.

fundamentals

Below are basic recipes for tart doughs, fruit curds, toppings, and garnishes that are called for in this book; they are also useful additions to any baker's repertory. The tips and techniques that follow will help you work efficiently and confidently with ingredients such as chocolate, citrus fruits, and egg whites. Master these dessert fundamentals and you will be well-equipped to create many delicious finales.

basic tartlet dough

1¼ cups all-purpose flour

1½ tablespoons sugar

¼ teaspoon salt

6 tablespoons cold unsalted butter, cut into ½-inch cubes

4–6 tablespoons ice water

In a food processor, combine the flour, sugar, and salt and pulse briefly. Add the butter and pulse until the mixture resembles coarse meal. Transfer the mixture to a large bowl. Using a fork, stir in 4 tablespoons of the ice water. The dough should start to come together into a rough mass. Squeeze a small piece of dough with your fingers; if it doesn't hold together without crumbling, stir in the remaining water, 1 tablespoon at a time. Gather the dough into a ball on a large sheet of plastic wrap. Press the dough into a disk, wrap tightly, and refrigerate until chilled and firm, at least 1 hour or up to 2 days. Makes enough dough for 24 miniature tartlets.

almond galette dough

1 large egg yolk

½ teaspoon almond extract

½ cup sliced almonds

2 cups all-purpose flour

3 tablespoons sugar

¼ teaspoon salt

¾ cup cold unsalted butter, cut into cubes

2 tablespoons cream cheese

4–6 tablespoons ice water

In a bowl, whisk together the egg yolk and almond extract. In a food processor, finely grind the almonds. Add the flour, sugar, and salt and pulse briefly. Add the butter and pulse briefly. Add the cream cheese and pulse until the mixture resembles coarse meal. Add the egg yolk mixture and pulse to combine. Transfer the mixture to a large bowl. Using a fork, stir in 4 tablespoons of the ice water to bring the dough together into a rough mass. Squeeze a small piece of dough; if it does not hold together without crumbling, stir in the remaining water, 1 tablespoon at a time. Gather the dough into a ball on a large sheet of plastic wrap. Press the dough into a disk, wrap tightly, and refrigerate for at least 1 hour or up to 2 days. Makes enough dough for one 10-inch galette.

cocoa tartlet dough

1¼ cups all-purpose flour

⅓ cup unsweetened Dutch-process cocoa powder, plus cocoa for dusting

½ teaspoon salt

6 tablespoons unsalted butter, cut into cubes, at room temperature

½ cup plus 2 tablespoons confectioners' sugar

1 large egg, lightly beaten

In a bowl, whisk together the flour, cocoa, and salt. In a food processor, combine the butter and sugar and process until blended. Add the flour mixture and process until almost combined, about 8 seconds. Scrape the sides of the bowl and pulse until the mixture resembles coarse meal. Add the egg and process until the dough comes together. Transfer the dough to a work surface dusted with cocoa and knead 2 or 3 times to bring the dough together; it will be very soft. Press the dough into a disk and use right away or wrap tightly and refrigerate for up to 2 days (be sure to bring the dough to room temperature before using). Makes enough dough for six 3-inch tartlets.

vanilla tart dough

2 large egg yolks

1 teaspoon pure vanilla extract

1½ cups all-purpose flour

¼ cup confectioners' sugar

3 tablespoons granulated sugar

½ teaspoon salt

10 tablespoons cold unsalted butter, cut into cubes

In a bowl, whisk together the egg yolks and vanilla. In a food processor, combine the flour, sugars, and salt and pulse briefly. Add the butter and process until the mixture resembles coarse meal. Add the yolk mixture and process until the dough comes together. Transfer to a lightly floured work surface and knead just to bring the dough together, then pat the dough into disk. Use right away. Makes enough dough for one 9½-inch tart.

basic galette dough

1 large egg yolk

½ teaspoon pure vanilla extract

2½ cups all-purpose flour

3 tablespoons sugar

¼ teaspoon salt

¾ cup cold unsalted butter, cut into cubes

2 tablespoons cream cheese

4–6 tablespoons ice water

In a bowl, whisk together the egg yolk and vanilla. In a food processor, combine the flour, sugar, and salt and pulse briefly. Add the butter and pulse briefly. Add the cream cheese and pulse until the mixture resembles coarse meal. Add the yolk mixture and pulse to combine. Transfer the mixture to a large bowl. Using a fork, stir in 4 tablespoons of the ice water to bring the dough together into a rough mass. Squeeze a small piece of dough; if it doesn't hold together without crumbling, stir in the remaining water, 1 tablespoon at a time. Gather the dough into a ball on a large sheet of plastic wrap. Press the dough into a disk, wrap tightly, and refrigerate for at least 1 hour or up to 2 days. Makes enough dough for one 10-inch galette.

passion fruit curd

4 fresh ripe passion fruits or ¼ cup thawed frozen passion fruit pulp

2 large egg yolks, at room temperature

⅓ cup sugar

pinch salt

3 tablespoons unsalted butter

Cut the passion fruits in half and scoop their pulp into a fine-mesh sieve set over a bowl. Press on the pulp to push it through the sieve and discard the seeds. Measure ¼ cup pulp and juice and add it to a nonreactive saucepan. Whisk in the egg yolks, sugar, and salt. Cook the mixture over medium-low heat, whisking constantly, until it thickens and turns a bright orange-yellow color (do not let the mixture boil), 2–3 minutes. Remove from the heat, whisk in the butter, and then strain through a fine-mesh sieve. Let cool for 15 minutes, then cover with plastic wrap, pressing it directly onto the surface of the curd. Refrigerate until cold, about 1½ hours. Makes about ¾ cup.

lemon curd

3 lemons

4 large eggs, at room temperature

1 cup sugar

pinch salt

4 tablespoons unsalted butter

2 tablespoons heavy cream

Finely grate 1 tablespoon zest from the lemons, then squeeze ½ cup lemon juice. Add both to a nonreactive saucepan. Whisk in the eggs, sugar, and salt. Cook the mixture over medium-low heat, whisking constantly, until it turns bright yellow and is thick enough to coat the back of a wooden spoon (do not let the mixture boil), 3–4 minutes. Remove from the heat, whisk in the butter followed by the cream, and then strain through a fine-mesh sieve. Let cool to room temperature. Use right away or cover with plastic wrap, pressing it directly onto the surface of the curd, and refrigerate for up to 3 days. Makes about 1¾ cups.

sherry–cream cheese frosting

½ pound cream cheese, at room temperature

¼ cup unsalted butter, at room temperature

pinch salt

⅔ cup confectioners' sugar, sifted

1 teaspoon dry sherry

Using a stand mixer on medium-high speed, beat the cream cheese, butter, and salt until light and creamy, 1–2 minutes. Add the sugar and beat until smooth. Mix in the sherry. Use right away. Makes about 1½ cups.

sweetened whipped cream

1 cup cold heavy cream

1 teaspoon pure vanilla extract

3 tablespoons sugar

Using a stand or handheld mixer on medium speed, whip the cream, vanilla, and sugar until frothy. Increase the speed to medium-high and continue to beat until the cream holds soft peaks, 1–2 minutes. Use right away. Makes about 2 cups.

candied citrus zest

1 grapefruit

1 orange

1 lemon

1½ cups sugar

Using a vegetable peeler and working from top to bottom, remove the zest from the each fruit in long, wide strips. Using a paring knife, scrape away any white pith from the undersides. Add the zest strips to a saucepan, cover with 1 inch of water, and bring to a boil. Drain and repeat, then place the zest strips on paper towels and blot dry.

In a saucepan, combine 1 cup of the sugar and 1 cup water. Add the zest strips and bring to a simmer over medium-high heat. Reduce the heat to low and cook, stirring occasionally, until the strips are translucent, 20–25 minutes. Pour the remaining ½ cup sugar into a bowl. Using a fork, lift the strips from the syrup, drain briefly, and transfer the strips to the sugar. Toss the strips in the sugar until evenly coated, then let dry on a plate. Makes about 20 pieces.

crème fraîche

1 cup heavy cream

1 tablespoon buttermilk

In a small saucepanover medium-low heat, combine the cream and buttermilk. Heat just until the mixture is lukewarm (do not allow the mixture to simmer).

Transfer the mixture to a nonreactive bowl, cover, and let stand at warm room temperature until thickened, at least 8 hours and up to 48 hours. Refrigerate until well chilled before using. Makes 1 cup.

getting ready to bake

Before making any recipe, especially a baking recipe that requires attention and precision, carefully read it through and make sure that all the necessary ingredients and equipment are on hand—don't be forced to rummage through the cupboard in the middle of mixing a cake batter! This is also the time to check if any of the ingredients require special preparation, such as cold eggs that need to be brought to room temperature or butter that needs to be melted and cooled. If the oven must be preheated or if baking pans must be greased, this is the time to do so.

preparing pans for baking

Every baker knows the disappointment of having a cake stick to its pan. Well-greased pans ensure that baked goods release easily after baking. Whether it's a nonstick or traditional baking pan, a generous coating of nonstick cooking spray or softened butter—not just a smear from the butter wrapper—is almost always a good precautionary measure. (In general, tart pans do not need to be greased because high-fat tart doughs typically do not stick to tart pans.) Lining baking sheets with parchment paper is also good practice, especially when baking free-form fruit tarts that release juices during baking. Parchment paper not only guarantees that the tart can be removed from the baking sheet once it's baked, it also simplifies clean up.

testing the oven's heat

Correct oven temperature is crucial when baking—a too-cool oven can result in under-risen and under-browned baked goods, while a too-hot oven can cause scorching. To test an oven's accuracy, place an oven thermometer in the center of the oven, turn on the oven, and allow it to heat thoroughly. If the oven is not calibrated with its heat setting, make the necessary adjustments by reducing or raising the heat. If the oven is known to have hot spots, which can cause baked goods to brown unevenly, rotating the pan or pans during baking can help them to achieve more even browning.

measuring ingredients

Correct measurement of ingredients is one of the keys to success when baking—even a small mismeasurement can have an adverse effect on a recipe. Dry ingredients and wet ingredients require different measuring tools and techniques.

dry ingredients Use sturdy dry measuring cups or spoons. Dip the measuring cup or spoon into the ingredient and scoop up a mound. Use a straight edge, such as an icing spatula or the back of a knife blade, to push off the excess and level the mound.

wet ingredients Use a liquid measuring cup, preferably one made of tempered glass. Fill the cup, allow the liquid to settle, and then gauge the measurement by bending down so that the cup is at eye level.

toasting nuts

Toasting nuts crisps their texture and lightly browns them, giving them a richer, fuller flavor. Be sure to let toasted nuts cool before using them in a recipe so that their natural fats do not cause clumping.

on the stove top Place the nuts in an even layer in a dry skillet. Toast the nuts over medium heat, stirring them often, until fragrant and lightly browned.

in the oven Scatter the nuts in an even layer in a baking dish or on a baking sheet. Toast them in a 325°F to 375°F oven until fragrant and lightly browned.

working with chocolate

Chocolate has a reputation as being a difficult ingredient to work with. The recipes in this book do not require fussy techniques, just a basic understanding of chocolate.

choosing When shopping, be sure to purchase the type of chocolate that the recipe calls for; unsweetened, bittersweet, semisweet, milk, and white chocolates all have distinct characteristics and flavors.

They also behave quite differently from each other when used in recipes, so it is important to use the right kind. For the richest, fullest flavor, purchase a high-quality chocolate, ideally from a store that quickly sells and replenishes its stock.

melting All types of chocolate are very sensitive to heat. To melt chocolate without causing it to "seize" (turn hard and gritty) or scorch, finely chop the chocolate and place it in a clean, dry heatproof bowl. Set the bowl over a saucepan containing about an inch of barely simmering water; the bottom of the bowl should not touch the simmering water. This setup is called a double boiler and is used to heat many temperature-sensitive foods. Let the chocolate melt slowly, stirring it occasionally with a clean spoon or heatproof spatula and taking care not to allow any moisture into the bowl. Once the chocolate is completely melted and smooth, remove the bowl from the saucepan.

storing In addition to being heat-sensitive, chocolate has a tendency to absorb aromas from other foods. To store chocolate, wrap it tightly in several layers of plastic wrap and place in a cool, dark spot away from fragrant foods such as onions and spices. If subjected to changes in temperature, chocolate sometimes blooms, or forms chalky white streaks. Chocolate that has bloomed has a texture that is unappealing on the palate, but it is perfectly fine for melting and use in recipes.

beating egg whites

Though whole eggs are easier to separate when they are cold, egg whites whip up more quickly when they are at room temperature. When beating egg whites, make sure that they are free from any bits of egg yolk and that bowl and whisk or whisk attachment are perfectly clean—even small traces of fat or oil will prevent the whites from achieving the proper volume and texture. Whipped egg whites must be used right away.

rolling out pastry dough

Pastry dough is easiest to roll out in a cool kitchen and when the dough itself is chilled and slightly malleable, not cold and hard. If the dough becomes soft and sticky during rolling, slide it onto or set it on a baking sheet and return it to the refrigerator to chill until it is once again workable.

1 Flour the work surface Lightly dust the work surface with flour, set the dough disk on the surface, and then dust the surface of the disk with flour.

2 Begin rolling Working from the center of the disk, roll outward to the edges in all directions, applying even pressure with the rolling pin.

3 Lift and rotate the dough To make sure that the dough is not sticking to the work surface, occasionally slide an icing spatula or bench scraper under the dough, then rotate the dough a quarter turn. Continue to roll until the round reaches the desired diameter.

using a hot water bath

Delicate, egg-rich cakes and custards are often baked in a water bath. The water acts as insulation during baking, protecting the perimeter of the cake or custard from overbaking as the center cooks through. Using a water bath requires some caution. First, set the filled cake pan or ramekins in a large roasting pan or baking dish. Then, fill a pitcher or large measuring cup with hot tap water. Transfer the roasting pan to the oven rack without jostling or spilling. Finally, very carefully pour the hot water into the pan without splashing, filling it as far as the recipe directs. When removing the pan from the oven, do so with care so that the water does not splash onto the dessert.

making caramel

Caramel's toasty, bittersweet flavor pairs well with many desserts.

1 Use a deep saucepan Choose a heavy saucepan that seems a little too large for the task. The pan's heft will help ensure that the sugar cooks evenly, and its size will contain the caramel mixture as it rises and bubbles vigorously when the cream is added.

2 Don't swirl or stir too often The sugar and water mixture is swirled or stirred in the initial stages of cooking, but once the sugar has dissolved, before it begins to take on color, the caramel should not be stirred. Stirring at this point introduces the risk of crystallization of the sugar into a dry, grainy mass.

3 Keep a close watch Once the sugar begins to color, it's safe to swirl the pan, but keep a close watch, because the caramel browns very quickly. if necessary, lower the heat under the saucepan and be prepared to remove the saucepan from the heat and add the cream to halt the cooking.

4 Add the cream carefully When the cream is added, the caramel mixture will sputter and bubble vigorously. Pour it in slowly, in several additions, if necessary, and then stir or whisk the mixture to incoporate the cream and dissolve any hardened bits of sugar.

making ice cream

Making ice cream or sorbet requires a little planning in advance. The ice cream base must be thoroughly chilled before being churned. In addition, many electric ice cream makers require that the canister used to churn the ice cream base be frozen for at least 24 hours prior to use. Check the manufacturer's instructions. Immediately after churning, it is a good idea to freeze the ice cream, with plastic wrap pressed directly on its surface, for a few hours to firm its texture.

working with citrus

Citrus fruits add bright flavor that works well with many other dessert components.

zesting If a recipe calls for both citrus zest and juice, zest the fruit before juicing because it is easier to zest when whole. To grate citrus zest, use a fine-toothed rasp-style grater. Using light pressure, move the citrus back and forth against the grater's teeth, removing only the rind and leaving behind the white pith, which is bitter tasting.

juicing To get the most juice from a citrus fruit, bring the fruit to room temperature and roll it back and forth along a work surface under the palm of your hand, applying firm pressure, so that the fruit softens slightly. Cut the fruit in half and use a citrus press or reamer to juice each half. Strain the juice to remove seeds or bits of pulp.

cutting into segments Slice off the top and bottom of the fruit, then set the fruit on one of the cut sides. Using a sharp, thin-bladed knife, cut the skin and white pith away in strips, following the rounded countour of the fruit. Work your way around the fruit, rotating it as needed. Hold the fruit in one hand. Working over a bowl to catch the juice and segments, cut along each side of the membrane that separates the segments and let the segments drop into the bowl as you work your way around the fruit.

working with pineapple

When selecting a pineapple, look for one that feels heavy for its size with vibrant green leaves. It should also have a fruity fragrance and be bruise-free. To remove its thick scaly skin, follow these steps.

1 Cut off the top and bottom Using a sharp knife, cut off the top and bottom of the fruit and stand it upright on a cut side.

2 Slice off the skin Working top to bottom, slice off the skin in wide strips. Cut deep enough to remove most of the eyes, but not too much of the flesh.

3 Cut out the eyes Using the tip of a paring knife, remove any remaining eyes. Cut the fruit into pieces and remove the core as directed in the recipe.

washing fresh berries

Fresh berries require delicate handling because they bruise very easily. To wash them, fill a large bowl with cool water. Empty the berries from their containers into the water and gently swish them about, picking out any that are bruised. Lift the berries out of the water by hand and set them in a single layer on a folded kitchen towel or triple-thickness of paper towels to dry. Wash berries just before use and use them right away; washed berries do not keep well.

hulling strawberries

Hull strawberries after washing them and just before use.

1 Insert a knife Insert the tip of a sharp paring knife at a slight angle just under the stem area until the tip of the knife reaches the center of the berry.

2 Pull off the top Cut around the stem area, rotating the berry to make a circular cut. Gently pull or pry off the top.

pitting stone fruits

Peaches, nectarines, apricots, plums, and pluots have large center pits, or stones. If the fruit is freestone, the flesh will easily seperate from the pit; if it is clinstone, the pit will take some effort to remove.

1 Cut the fruit in half Cut the fruit in half from pole to pole, working around the pit, and then separate the halves. If they do not separate easily, gently twist them apart.

2 Remove the pit Using the tip of a paring knife, pry out the pit. If it is firmly attached to the flesh, use the tip of a paring knife to cut under and around it and cut it free.

seasonal ingredients

This chart will help you know, at a glance, the seasonality of the produce used in this book, along with a few extras thrown in for good measure. Some fruits, such as apples, have peak seasons that are indicated in the chart though they are available year-round; many imported tropical fruits are also available all year. Solid dots indicate peak seasons; open dots indicate transitional seasons.

INGREDIENTS	SPRING	SUMMER	FALL	WINTER
apples			●	○
apricots	●	○		
asian pears			●	●
bananas	●	●	●	●
basil	○	●	○	
bay leaves, fresh	●	●	●	●
blackberries		●		
blood oranges				●
blueberries		●		
cantaloupe		●	○	
cherries, sour		●		
cherries, sweet		●		
corn		●	○	
cranberries			●	○
figs		●	●	
ginger	●	●	●	●
grapefruit	○			●
honeydew		●	○	
key limes	●	●		
kiwifruit	●			●
lemons	●	●	●	●

INGREDIENTS	SPRING	SUMMER	FALL	WINTER
lemongrass	●	●	●	●
limes	○			●
mango	●	●	●	●
meyer lemons	○			●
nectarines		●	○	
oranges	●	●	●	●
passion fruit	●	●	●	●
peaches		●	○	
pears			●	●
persimmons			●	●
pineapple	●	●	●	●
plums		●	○	
pluots		●	○	
pumpkin			●	●
quince			●	
raspberries	●	●	○	
rhubarb	●	●		
rosemary	●	●	●	●
strawberries	●	●		
tangerines			○	●
watermelon		●	○	

glossary

amaretti These small, light, very crisp Italian macaroons flavored with bitter almonds sometimes come individually wrapped. They can be found in well-stocked markets and Italian specialty stores.

amaretto A deep golden liqueur with a sweet and mildly bitter taste, amaretto is infused with flavor of bitter almonds.

arrowroot The starch derived from the root a tropical plant, arrowroot is used as a thickening agent. It is sold as a fine white powder that is tasteless and colorless when cooked.

Asian pears There are numerous varieties of these fruits, which resemble a cross between apples and pears. They range widely in color and size, but a juicy, crisp, slightly granular texture and sweet, fruity flavor is characteristic of all Asian pears.

baking powder A leavening agent for baked goods, baking powder consists of baking soda, an acid, and a stabilizer. Liquid, and, in the case of double-acting baking powder, heat, activates the baking powder, releasing carbon dioxide gas, causing the batter to rise.

baking soda Baking soda is a powdery white alkali whose reaction to acidic ingredients, such as buttermilk or sour cream, creates carbon dioxide gas, causes batters to rise.

balsamic vinegar A sweet-sour taste and dark reddish brown color characterize balsamic vinegar. Made from the cooked must of Trebbiano grapes, true balsamic vinegar comes from the Emilia-Romagna region of Italy. The longer the vinegar ages, the more viscous and valuable it becomes.

basmati rice Basmati rice is an aromatic long-grain rice with a very nutty flavor and fragrance. It is the favored rice of India and parts of the Middle East.

bay leaves, fresh The green-gray leaves of the laurel tree, bay leaves have a savory herbal fragrance. At one time, dried bay was the only type available, but fresh bay leaves, which have a more delicate and complex flavor than dried, have become quite common in grocery stores.

biscotti, almond This very crunchy, mildly sweet, twice-baked Italian cookie is often served alongside a cup of coffee or a glass of dessert wine. Its texture and neutral flavor make it a good candidate for use in cookie crumb crusts.

blood orange This orange variety with distinctive red or red-streaked flesh has a sweet, yet tart, and slightly bitter flavor.

bourbon An American-made whiskey with a corn base, bourbon is aged in charred oak barrels, which gives the spirit its deep golden color and smoky flavor.

brandy This spirit is distilled from wine or fermented fruit juice that has been aged in wood, which adds both color and flavor.

brioche A classic French bread made with generous amounts of butter, milk, and eggs, brioche is characterized by a thin, deep golden brown crust and a fine, tender, cake-like crumb.

brown butter Called *beurre noisette* in French, which translates to "hazelnut butter," brown butter is plain butter that has been gently cooked until it takes on a light brown color and tastes and smells of hazelnuts. It is used in both sweet and savory dishes.

butter, unsalted Unsalted butter, which is sometimes labeled as sweet butter on the packaging, has not been seasoned with salt during its manufacture, giving the cook or baker full control over the amount of salt that is added to a recipe.

buttermilk In earlier times, buttermilk was the milky liquid that remained after cream was churned into butter. Today, it is made by adding a bacterial culture to milk, giving it a tangy flavor and thick texture.

caramel The result of cooking sugar until it browns and takes on a toasty, bittersweet flavor, caramel is used in both sweet and savory preparations. Caramel to which liquid has not been added will become hard and brittle upon cooling; caramel to which liquid (often cream or water) has been added will be viscous and pourable, depending on how much liquid is added.

cardamom A relative of ginger, cardamom is sold ground and as whole pods. The papery pods house tiny seeds that are the source of cardamom's warm, sweet flavor. When using pods, first crush them to expose the seeds; be sure to remove the pods before serving.

cayenne pepper A very hot red pepper made from ground dried cayenne chiles, cayenne is used sparingly to add heat or to heighten flavor.

Champagne, rosé This Champagne acquires a pale pink or peach hue from being exposed to the skins of red grapes or being blended with a small amount of red wine. Rosé Champagne has a slightly fuller flavor and body than regular Champagne.

cheese Cheese adds unique flavor and texture to many dishes, including desserts. To ensure freshness, try to purchase cheese from a specialty cheese shop and store it wrapped in paper instead of plastic.

blue Blue cheeses have been treated with mold and have formed bluish veins or pockets of mold that give the cheese its strong, piquant flavor. They range in texture from dry and crumbly to soft and creamy.

cream This fresh, unripened cheese, an American creation and an ingredient in cheesecake, has a tangy, salty flavor and a creamy, spreadable texture.

goat, fresh Also called chèvre, this pure white cheese is made from goat's milk and has a soft texture and a pleasantly tangy, slightly salty flavor. Do not use aged goat cheese in a recipe calling for fresh.

mascarpone A very soft, smooth, fresh Italian cheese made from cream, mascarpone is noted for its rich, buttery flavor and light tang and can be found sold in tubs in well-stocked grocery stores and Italian delicatessens.

Neufchâtel Traditionally a soft cheese from Normandy, France, Neufchâtel, in its American form, is a lower-fat alternative to cream cheese. Its slightly higher moisture content gives it a very spreadable texture.

ricotta Traditionally, ricotta is made by recooking the whey that is leftover from the production of cheese. It has a milky, mild flavor and moist, curdy texture.

Chinese five-spice powder This blend of five spices includes cinnamon, cloves, star anise, Szechuan peppercorns, and fennel or anise seeds. In some versions, ground ginger takes the place of one of the other spices.

chocolate There are many varieties of chocolate on store shelves; only the ones used in this book are discussed below.

bittersweet Mildly sweet bittersweet chocolate is made in a range of cocoa percentages; the higher the percentage, the less sweet and more bitter the chocolate. For the best results with the recipes in this book, use good-quality bittersweet chocolate with about 70 percent cocoa.

unsweetened Unsweetened chocolate is bitter and intensely flavored, such that it cannot be eaten out of hand. When used in a recipe, it must be balanced with a generous quantity of sugar.

unsweetened Dutch-process cocoa powder Basically, cocoa powder is unsweetened chocolate from which all the fat has been removed and has then been finely ground. Dutch-process cocoa has been treated with alkali to temper the cocoa's natural acidity, which also gives it a darker color.

white White chocolate is not a true chocolate, but rather cocoa butter and milk solids that are sweetened with sugar and flavored with vanilla. Its value is mostly in its smooth, buttery texture and its ability to support the other flavors in a dessert.

coconut The fruit of a tropical palm, coconuts have many culinary uses. Two types of coconut products are used in this book.

unsweetened coconut flakes Coconut flakes are shaved into large, wide shreds from the white inner meat of the coconut and are then dried. Look for them in natural-foods stores or Asian markets.

unsweetened coconut milk Sold in cans, coconut milk is made by processing grated coconut meat and water. Upon standing, the coconut fat rises to the surface of the milk, so, before use, shake the can or stir the contents well.

cream, heavy Of all the dairy products, heavy cream, which contains between 36 and 40 percent milk fat, is, by far, the richest. It is sometimes labeled as heavy whipping cream. For the best flavor, look for heavy cream that has been pasteurized but not ultra-pasteurized.

cream of tartar This white powder is potassium tartrate, an acidic by-product of wine making. It is added in very small amounts to egg whites before whipping to help create a stable and voluminous egg foam.

crème fraîche In the French tradition, crème fraîche is unpasteurized cream thickened by bacteria that is naturally present in the cream. More commonly, though, it is cream thickened by a bacteria that is added, yielding a soft, spreadable consistency and a tangy, slightly nutty flavor. Crème fraîche is sold in tubs, often in the specialty-cheese case.

crystallized ginger Sometimes called candied ginger, crystallized ginger is made by cooking ginger in a sugar syrup and then coating it with coarse sugar crystals. It is usually sold in thin slices.

Earl Grey tea This black tea gets its distinctive citrusy flavor and aroma from the oil of bergamot, a type of bitter orange.

fleur de sel *See Salt.*

flour Flour gives baked goods substance and structure. Below are the two types used in this book.

all-purpose As its name implies, this kitchen staple is a good flour for general use. Made from a blend of soft and hard wheats, it has a moderate protein content.

cake Cake flour is milled from soft wheat, giving it a low protein content and fine texture. It is used for baking cakes with tender, delicate crumbs.

galette This French term refers to many different types of flat, round cakes or baked goods, but, in this country, it is the name often given to rustic free-form tarts.

gelatin, unflavored Gelatin is a tasteless and colorless protein that is used as a thickening agent in both sweet and savory dishes. Before use, gelatin must first be soaked in liquid and then gently heated so that it dissolves smoothly.

Grand Marnier Deep golden in color, Grand Marnier is a Cognac-based French liqueur flavored with the dried peels of bitter oranges.

granita A simple frozen dessert, granita is made by freezing a fruit purée or flavored liquid and stirring the mixture occasionally as it solidifies to break up the ice crystals. The finished texture is coarse and granular.

jasmine tea To create this fragrant tea, green or oolong tea leaves are scented and flavored with jasmine flower petals. Brewed jasmine tea has a fresh, floral flavor.

juniper berries The dried bluish-black seeds of an evergreen, juniper berries, the flavoring in gin, have a slightly resinous flavor, and a fresh, piney quality. They are often used to season meats and game.

Key limes Named for the Florida Keys, Key limes are smaller than regular limes— sometimes as small as walnuts—and have a yellowish tinge to their skins. They have a sharp acidity and a slightly floral flavor.

kirsch Also known as kirschwasser, this clear brandy of German origin is made from cherries.

ladyfingers These light, sponge cake–style cookies are shaped like thick fingers. Crisp, dry ladyfingers, called *savoiardi,* can be found in well-stocked grocery stores and Italian specialty markets.

lemon oil This intense flavoring contains lemon flavor, without acidity. Look for lemon oil that has been pressed directly from lemon peels rather than oil that has been infused with lemon flavor.

lemongrass This herb with a fresh lemon flavor, but with none of lemon's brassiness, resembles a green onion with pale gray-green leaves. The tender inner core contains the most flavor.

macadamia nuts Native to Australia, macadamia nuts have a sweet, buttery flavor and a slightly waxy texture due to their high fat content. The nuts are almost always sold shelled because their casings are hard to crack.

Madeira This fortified wine from Portugal is aged using an unusual process of heating the wine, a step that contributes to Madeira's distinctive flavor. There are several varieties of Madeira, ranging from pale golden and lightly dry to dark and very sweet.

maple syrup Maple syrup is made by boiling down the sap of the sugar maple tree to an amber-colored syrup. The syrup is graded according to color, with the darkest syrups, labeled grade B or cooking maple, having the most robust flavor.

Meyer lemon Believed to be a cross between a regular lemon and a mandarin orange, Meyer lemons are thin-skinned and turn deep orangish yellow when ripe. Their fragrant juice and flesh are sweeter and less acidic than regular lemons.

molasses, dark Molasses is a by-product of sugar-cane processing. Dark molasses, which falls between light and blackstrap in the molasses spectrum, has a coffee-like color, a thick, syrupy texture, and a smoky, bitter, mildly sweet flavor.

moscato d'Asti This lightly sparkling Italian wine is made from the muscat grape. Sweet and low in alcohol, it is usually sipped as a dessert wine.

nonreactive Untreated aluminum or cast iron pans can react with acidic ingredients such as citrus juice, vinegar, or wine, giving them a metallic flavor and an off color. When in doubt, choose stainless steel, anodized aluminum, or enameled cast iron for pans cooking or stainless steel, glass, or ceramic bowls for mixing acidic mixtures.

oats, quick-cooking rolled To make this type of oats, oat groats are cut, steamed, and then rolled, yielding grain particles that have a hearty, chewy texture that will cook quickly in liquid.

orange-flower water The blossoms of bitter oranges are distilled to create this clear, highly perfumed flavoring that is often used in Middle Eastern cooking.

parchment paper A boon to any baker, parchment paper is resistant to heat, moisture, and even grease; it ensures the easy release of baked goods and simplifies clean up. When baking, do not substitute waxed paper, which is not heat-resistant.

passion fruit An egg-shaped tropical fruit with an intense sweet-tart flavor, passion fruit turns from smooth to wrinkly when ripe. The most common variety of passion fruit sold in stores is deep purple in color. The spoonable yellow pulp contains black seeds that are edible, but are often strained out. Frozen passion fruit purée can sometimes be found in Latin American markets.

Pavlova This classic dessert consists of a crisp baked meringue topped with whipped cream and fruits. Australian in origin, it is named for Anna Pavlova, a Russian ballerina that captivated Australian audiences in the early twentieth century.

persimmons Originally cultivated in China, persimmons are commonly available in two varieties. Red-orange, acorn-shaped Hachiya persimmons must be soft and fully ripened in order for the fruit to lose its astringency and be edible. Flatter, lighter-colored Fuyu persimmons have a crisp texture and are popular for eating out of hand.

pluot A twentieth-century fruit, pluots are a hybrid of plums and apricots. Largely plum in parentage, they are smooth-skinned, juicy, and have a plum-like flesh and flavor. Many varieties are available with skins and flesh that range in color.

Port True Port, a sweet fortified wine with jammy, concentrated flavors, hails from Portugal. There a few different varieties of Port, but for cooking, purchase a reasonably priced ruby or tawny Port, rather than an expensive vintage Port.

pot de crème From the French meaning "pot of cream," this rich, pudding-like custard dessert is traditionally made and served, chilled, in small lidded pots.

pumpkin purée This thick, unflavored purée of cooked pumpkin, sometimes simply labeled as pumpkin, is sold in cans. When buying, take care not to mistake pumpkin pie filling, which is seasoned with spices, for pumpkin purée.

quince A fruit that resembles a cross between and apple and pear in both flavor and appearance, quinces are golden yellow in color when ripe and have a floral fragrance. When raw, their flesh is firm, tart, and astringent; with cooking, it becomes tender, sweet, and mellow.

rhubarb Rhubarb stalks resemble bright pink or red celery stalks. They are the only edible portion of the rhubarb plant; the leaves are toxic. Rhubarb's fruity flavor is intensely tart and requires cooking with a generous amount of sugar to render it palatable.

Riesling Riesling, a complexly flavored white wine made from Riesling grapes, has a flavor profile that ranges from dry to very sweet. Most Rieslings, however, are notable for their delicately fruity and floral character.

rum Distilled from sugarcane juice or molasses, this slightly sweet spirit comes in several different varieties. Below are the types that are used in this book.

dark Deep amber in color and medium-bodied, dark rum is aged, which gives it woodsy caramel-like flavor notes.

spiced dark Medium golden brown in color and medium-bodied, spiced dark rum is flavored with a variety of warm spices.

white White rum is clear in color and has a very light flavor and body.

salt Arguably the most important seasoning, salt heightens the flavors of any dish, including desserts, and can add textural interest. The following are salt varieties used in this book.

flaky sea salt The texture of this salt is quite coarse and pleasantly crunchy. The salt grains are thin, flaky, and sometimes shaped like flattened pyramids.

fleur de sel This coarse, hand-harvested sea salt is a specialty of France. It has a moist texture and a complex, mineral-rich flavor.

salt Regular table salt is an all-purpose salt. Its fine crystals disperse and dissolve easily, making it the choice for many baking recipes.

sherry A fortified wine originating in Southern Spain, sherry is made from the Palomino Fino grape and comes in varieties that range in color and sweetness. Sherry is usually sipped as an aperitif or a dessert wine.

sour cherries Too tart to eat out of hand, but full of fruity flavor, sour cherries are the type of cherry that is commonly used in desserts and in preserves.

star anise These deep brown star-shaped pods have a flavor much like that of their namesake, anise seed, but with a more savory and assertive quality. They are native to China and, ground into powder, are a component in Chinese five-spice powder.

steamed pudding mold This tall metal vessel usually has fluted sides, a decorative bottom, and a lid that clamps into place. Steamed puddings are cooked in the upside-down mold, then inverted for serving.

streusel A crumbly mixture of butter, flour, sugar, and, often, spices, streusel is sometimes sprinkled onto unbaked cakes, muffins, and quick breads. With baking it becomes an appealingly crisp, brown topping.

sugar Sugar in an indispensable ingredient in the preparation of desserts. It adds sweetness and moisture, has tenderizing properties, and helps foods caramelize.

brown Rich in flavor, brown sugar is granulated sugar mixed with molasses. It has a soft, moist texture and comes in light brown and dark brown varieties.

confectioners' Also called powdered sugar, confectioners' sugar is granulated sugar that has been pulverized to a fine powder and combined with a small amount of cornstarch to prevent clumping.

granulated The most common sugar is white granulated sugar, which has been extracted from sugarcane or beets. For baking, buy only cane sugar, as beet sugar may have an unpredictable effect on recipes.

superfine Superfine sugar, sometimes called bar sugar, is granulated sugar that has been very finely ground. Because the granules are so tiny, superfine sugar readily dissolves, making it the preferred sugar for uncooked or cold recipes.

turbinado A raw, coarse-grained sugar, turbinado sugar is made by steaming unrefined sugar. It has a light golden color and hints of molasses flavor.

summer pudding A classic English summertime dessert consists of a bread-lined bowl or dish filled with lightly cooked fresh berries. It is then topped with more bread and weighted for several hours in the refrigerator. The "pudding" is unmolded for serving.

tapioca, large pearl Made from the root of the cassava plant, pearl tapioca is sold in various sizes. Orbs of uncooked large pearl tapioca are about the size of peas. When cooked, they have a pleasantly chewy texture. Large pearl tapioca is sold in well-stocked grocery stores and Asian markets.

torte A torte is a cake made with little or no flour. It is usually very rich and dense and is often served with an accompaniment that offsets these traits.

trifle This traditional English dessert of sponge cake or ladyfingers soaked with spirits and layered into a deep bowl along with custard or pastry cream, fruits, and whipped cream, has the best flavor after the components have had a chance to meld for a few hours.

vanilla beans The cured, dried seed pods of a tropical orchid, vanilla beans are the source of the richest, purest vanilla essence. When buying, look for beans that are plump, shiny, and moist, all good indicators of freshness. The brown, wrinkly bean must be split open and the seeds scraped out to release its flavor. They are sold in well-stocked markets and in specialty food stores.

vanilla extract, pure This clear brown flavoring is made by steeping vanilla beans in alcohol. Avoid imitation vanilla extract which is made without vanilla beans and lacks the complexity of pure extract.

yogurt, Greek-style This plain yogurt, made in the style of traditional Greek yogurt, has a thick, creamy texture and a rich, tangy flavor. If it is not available, a reasonable substitute can be made by placing plain whole-milk yogurt in a cheesecloth-lined fine-mesh sieve and allowing it to drain for a few hours.

zabaglione A rich Italian custard made from egg yolks, sugar, and wine (traditionally Marsala), zabaglione has a light, frothy texture as can be served on its own or as a dessert accompaniment. It is sometimes called by its French name, *sabayon*.

index

OXMOOR HOUSE

Oxmoor House books are distributed by Sunset Books
80 Willow Road, Menlo Park, CA 94025
Telephone: 650 324 1532
VP and Associate Publisher Jim Childs
Director of Marketing Sydney Webber
Oxmoor House and Sunset Books are divisions
of Southern Progress Corporation

WILLIAMS-SONOMA, INC.
Founder & Vice-Chairman Chuck Williams

WILLIAMS-SONOMA NEW FLAVORS SERIES
Conceived and produced by Weldon Owen Inc.
415 Jackson Street, Suite 200, San Francisco, CA 94111
Telephone: 415 291 0100 Fax: 415 291 8841
www.weldonowen.com

In Collaboration with Williams-Sonoma, Inc.
3250 Van Ness Avenue, San Francisco, CA 94109

A WELDON OWEN PRODUCTION
Copyright © 2008 Weldon Owen Inc. and Williams-Sonoma, Inc.
All rights reserved, including the right of reproduction
in whole or in part in any form.

First printed in 2008
Printed in Singapore

10 9 8 7 6 5 4 3 2 1
Library of Congress Cataloging-in-Publication Data is available.

ISBN-13: 978-0-8487-3255-4
ISBN-10: 0-8487-3255-3

This book is printed with paper harvested from well-managed forests
utilizing sustainable and environmentally sound practices.

WELDON OWEN INC.

Executive Chairman, Weldon Owen Group John Owen
CEO and President, Terry Newell
Senior VP, International Sales Stuart Laurence
VP, Sales and New Business Development Amy Kaneko
Director of Finance Mark Perrigo

VP and Publisher Hannah Rahill
Executive Editor Jennifer Newens
Senior Editor Dawn Yanagihara
Associate Editor Julia Humes

VP and Creative Director Gaye Allen
Art Director Kara Church
Senior Designer Ashley Martinez
Designer Stephanie Tang
Photo Manager Meghan Hildebrand

Production Director Chris Hemesath
Production Manager Michelle Duggan
Color Manager Teri Bell

Photographers Tucker + Hossler
Food Stylist Erin Quon
Prop Stylist Chuck Luter

Additional Photography Kate Sears: pages 54, 84, 91, 113; Dan Goldberg:
pages 62, 105, 106; Rachel Weill: page 139; Getty Images: Dennis Gottlieb,
pages 14–15, Image Source, pages 78–79, Paul Katz, page 107; Corbis: pages
46–47, Bill Barksdale, pages 110–111; Shutterstock: Marie C. Fields, page 131;
Jupiter Images: Burke/Triolo Productions, page 139.

ACKNOWLEDGMENTS

Weldon Owen wishes to thank the following individuals for their kind
assistance: Food Stylist Assistants Jeffrey Larsen and Victoria Woollard; Photo
Consultant Andrea Stephany; Copy editor Heather Belt; Proofreader Carrie
Bradley; Indexer Ken DellaPenta.